From Good to G.R.E.A.T. (Second Edition)

© 2015 Molesey Crawford

ISBN: 978-0-578-05683-8

Editing of the Original Manuscript
C & K Publishing

Logo Design
Graphic Designs Unlimited

Interior Layout
Abiola Sholanke of Rainbow Creative Group

Interior Artwork via VectorStock

Copies of this book may be obtained at
www.thequeencode.com.

From Good To
G.R.E.A.T.

33 Days to Unlocking Your Greatest Potential & Living the Life of Your Dreams

By Molesey Crawford

This book is dedicated to those who dream big dreams

and have the vision to make the impossible possible.

When there's no door for opportunity to knock, we will

build one.

And to those who dare to think outside the box and find

that God is there too…

The future belongs to us.

Contents

Part III: Be Empowered

Part IV: Be Authentic

Part V: Trust Divine Timing

Introduction

If you always thought there was more to life than your current existence, then you're right. All my life I've been reaching and searching for something better than my surroundings. My search has led me on a journey with high highs and low lows; twists and turns, and many times a complete circle back to where I started.

I learned along the way that life is a never-ending course in personal development. Those of us who understand this fact and embrace it experience extraordinary transformation because we are aligning

> *"... life is a never-ending course in personal development."*

ourselves with Divine purpose. You see, to realize our highest potential is our greatest work. To believe that there is more to who you are, and to follow your heart to find the keys to the kingdom is a noble pursuit.

In today's world, finding a person who is living the life of their dreams is uncommon. It is more common to experience life on an earn-and-consume treadmill or in lack, disappointment, disharmony, strife, and contention. But the world is changing. Today, we find ourselves in the midst of a Universal shift and an evolution in consciousness. We are experiencing the rebirth of the feminine principle which brings an intense, growing desire for meaning and fulfillment, peace, understanding, healing, and freedom from mental and spiritual bondage. We are finally awakening from our slumber. The scales are falling away from our eyes as we remember who we are and the possibility of who we can be.

Upon graduating from college in 2005, I set out to fulfill many of my dreams, one of which was writing a book. I found my passion for writing when I was 10. I started out writing children's books and by my teenage years I had evolved to poems and then songs for the girl group my friends and I started. In college, writing was reserved for term papers and senior thesis work, but with my undergraduate degree in hand I had the opportunity to express myself freely once again. I learned from Maya Angelou that "a bird sings because it has a song." At that point in my life, I had experienced a great deal, and I had a lot to say...so I began writing.

Within four years I started four manuscripts, but failed to finish one. Then one day in May of 2009 as I was sitting on my front porch, I received inspiration for what would be the fifth book started, but the first one completed. It was a beautiful sunny day, but I was feeling a little depressed. I was preparing for one of the biggest events of my life and getting ready was an uphill battle. I was trying to build a better future for myself, but to do that I had to face the demons of my past and present. I was in the midst of the Refiner's fire and the heat was to the max. A Voice from within said, "Everything that you are going through now and everything that you've been through to get to this point in your life, write it down. You are about to go to a new place. You are about to go from good to great. This is your first book."

Once a butterfly emerges from its cocoon, it never goes back to being a caterpillar. There was an evolution happening and I could sense that I would never be the same. So I did as I was told with no hesitation. I began to document the movement. Over the next five months I recorded every trial, every struggle, every memory of past obstacles and how I overcame them, every "Divine download" and inspirational thought. By October, I had dozens of pages in a Word document and several pages of notes in my iPhone. From there I started my first draft. Within another five months, the work was completed.

This book is for those who are ready for accelerated growth in their lives. Over the next 33 days we will uncover the tools and characteristics needed to live the life of your dreams. From all the things I've experienced, I have come to the conclusion that to live a great life you must:

Operate in your God-given purpose

Be Resilient

Be Empowered

Be Authentic

And Trust Divine Timing

I chose the number 33 because it is a Divine number that represents the completion of a journey and ascension to a higher level of living. A great example would be the life and legacy of Jesus the Christ. For the book cover I chose colors that represent the goal of this adventure. Green for positive energy, life, vitality, health, prosperity and growth. Purple for regality, power, and living in high material places; and a dazzling gold which represents completeness and living in high spiritual places. Pure gold is a gift to those who overcome and persevere.

The course of this book is an excellent time for self-discovery. Take each day as a challenge to uncover something new within yourself. This is your time to come face-to-face with where you are and build a foundation for the success you desire

"Take each day as a challenge to uncover something new within yourself."

to have. I realized that it's important to understand success because if you don't "get it" you'll never have it. The key to success is to live your life as if no one owes you anything. Feelings of entitlement will hold you back. You must embrace personal responsibility if want to achieve excellence because no one else holds the key to your fulfillment. If you are not living the life of your dreams, it's up to YOU to change that.

At the end of each chapter, you will receive one of "33 Principles To A G.R.E.A.T. Life." Use these as guides to evaluate your progress, strengths, and areas of opportunity. You may find that you resonate with some chapters more than others. I share my personal stories with the prayer that something I've gone through may bring encouragement and light to your situation.

Contrary to popular belief, the sky is NOT the limit. *The best kept secret of life is that there are no limits*. The only limits that ever exist are the ones we create in our minds.

Taking the boundaries off ourselves is a lifelong process, but with every chain we break away from our minds, we are empowered. You have the amazing opportunity to experience more freedom today by stepping outside of your comfort zone and expanding your mind with the principles in this book. It doesn't matter who you are, where you are from, or what you've been through. You may be at a point in your life where the only place you can find inspiration is in the dictionary. You have all you need to move forward now. Everything you need to grow and develop is within.

Years ago when I began to embrace my spirituality, I asked God the true meaning of life and the reason for our existence. The answer came back to me in a flash: *To spread Love and Light.* His words set me free, and I realized that salvation is always found in the simple Truth. When we live our true purpose, we bring Love and Light into the world in the capacity that fits us best. It would be selfish to allow fear and ignorance to restrain you from giving the world what it needs from you. Grow the courage and get the knowledge you need to boldly pursue your life's purpose. Commit yourself to these principles for the next 33 days and watch your life transform.

Love & Light,

From Good to G.R.E.A.T.

PART I:

Operate In Your G̲od-Given Purpose

From Good to G.R.E.A.T.

Day 1

Embracing Our True Nature

"You will never feel more alive than when you
live the dream God created for you."

– Mary J. Blige

When I was a little girl, I would look up at the stars in amazement and ask a thousand questions about the meaning of life. Many years later as a young adult I continued to ask the same questions. The truth is, at some point in time we all wonder: What is life really all about? And, why am I here? I realized that the overall purpose of life can be found in the first four words God ever spoke to humankind. Upon the completion of man and woman, He said to them, "Be fruitful and multiply" (Genesis 1:28). In essence, our first command was to expand. The Almighty intended for humankind to be prosperous, abundant and above all, to *grow*. Not just

19

physically through procreation, but in every area of our existence.

But what about you, specifically? What is *your* purpose? We all have talents that are intrinsically connected to our purpose. Look over your life. What can you do better than anyone else? What are the things that come easiest to you or the activities that you could do all day and never get tired? What makes you happy? What do you desire to do or be? What sets you on fire? Living your purpose should come as natural to you as breathing. It's not just second nature; it's your *true* nature.

> "We were meant to live an effective and meaningful life, free of mundane tasks."

We can't reach our highest potential without finding our rightful place in the Universe. We were meant to live an effective and meaningful life, free of mundane tasks. By embracing our purpose, we can shift from surviving to thriving. As we move into adulthood, we may find it difficult to retain our ability to dream. But our purpose can be found dancing on the playground of our dreams and imagination. It's time to *believe* again. As you open your mind, you will begin to realize that you are joint heir to a world of infinite possibilities. Living a life of passion, fulfillment and abundance is your birthright.

Unfortunately, many people have allowed themselves to stop reaching higher after failed attempts at living their dreams. Instead of boldly pursuing their passions they "bargain with life for a penny." But one of the main desires of our Spirit is to seek greater expression. If you listen closely, our Spirit yearns for a deeper, meaningful life. Like a whisper in the wind, It speaks with a quiet voice, and if we listen, It can lead us to what we've ultimately desired. The Voice, like a compass, points to the way. Surprisingly, it's not east or west, north or south. The Way is within.

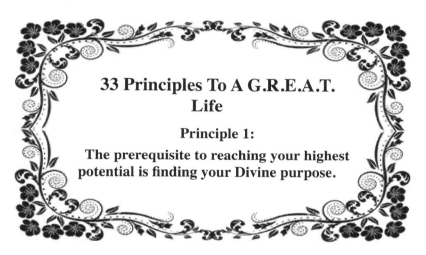

33 Principles To A G.R.E.A.T. Life

Principle 1:

The prerequisite to reaching your highest potential is finding your Divine purpose.

Day 2

The Kingdom Within

"Now when He was asked by the Pharisees when the kingdom of God would come, He answered them and said, "The kingdom of God does not come with observation; nor will they say, 'See here!' or 'See there!' For indeed, the kingdom of God is within you."

– Luke 17:20-21

"But seek first the kingdom of God and His righteousness, and all these things shall be added to you."

– Matthew 6:33

22

The most essential part to living a great life is seeking first the kingdom within. This should be your first priority daily. Connecting with the Source will bring clarity to your life and reveal your purpose. Generally, we connect through prayer when we talk to God, and meditation when we listen to Him. This is the one place where we cannot cut corners. In the past, I have been repeatedly guilty of jumping out of bed and leaping straight into life. But we must seek the kingdom within *first*. It will set the tone for our day. Even if you have to set your alarm for 4 a.m. when the house is quiet to pray and meditate, stretch yourself and do it. If you want something great, a greater price must be paid.

To understand why you were created, who better to consult than the Creator! Peeling back the layers to reach your core may be a rough process, but the best treasures are found in deep places. Like a diver who goes to the depths of a vast ocean to find a valuable pearl, you must be willing to explore and go the distance for something much better than a pearl, a truly priceless treasure: the knowledge of who you really are and the God-given power you have to be great.

"Seeking the Kingdom within nourishes and sustains a great life."

Real power is spiritual and originates from within you. That's why I believe that the most important time you'll ever spend is in silence. Silence feeds the soul and recharges your battery. Think about a cell phone. If you charge it for 10 minutes, you may be able to use it for 30 minutes or so before it needs more power. Just like an electrical gadget, the power you manifest will always be in direct proportion to how often you charge your battery or stay connected to the power Source.

Seeking the Kingdom within nourishes and sustains a great life. It elevates your state of mind and gives you the right perspective. It allows you to go beyond the superficial to develop a deeper understanding. You begin to see meaning in things that others see as meaningless. Going within not only creates an awareness of who we are, but also reveals the steps to take to become who we are meant to be. I always say that the Spirit within us knows how great we are, and It is trying to get us to remember.

Our lives manifest like a slide projector. Whatever is on the inside projects larger on the outside. Once you place the film or disk inside a projector it is no longer visible, but it is responsible for what you view on a larger scale. A person conflicted on the inside experiences conflict on the outside. A person

"... it's a frivolous pursuit to look for peace, happiness, and fulfillment on the outside."

who rehearses negativity and past offenses on the inside finds themselves in negative situations throughout their life. That's why it's a frivolous pursuit to look for peace, happiness, and fulfillment on the outside. *Change always happens first in the Spirit realm.*

Even the people of Jesus' day had the issue of looking

for greatness outside of themselves in the material world. They were literally looking for the "kingdom" complete with earthly mansions and high-ranking positions. But like the classic movie about self-realization, *The Wizard of Oz*, you won't find your greatness "somewhere over the rainbow." In the end you'll realize what you've been searching for all along was inside of you.

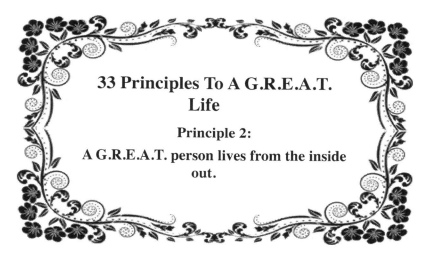

33 Principles To A G.R.E.A.T. Life

Principle 2:

A G.R.E.A.T. person lives from the inside out.

Day 3

The Vision

"For the vision is yet for an appointed time, but at the end it shall speak and not lie. Though it tarry, wait for it, because it will surely come; it will not tarry."

– Habakkuk 2:3

On a chilly evening in December of 2004, I had an experience that would change my life forever. We'll call it: The Vision. I was kneeling at my bedside, reflecting on that year and anticipating the New Year bringing better things. 2004 had been a period of major transformation for me. I had gotten serious about cultivating my spirituality. I cut off unhealthy relationships. I even exercised my right to vote for the first time in the 2004 presidential races. It was also the first year since living on my own at the age of 18 that I had financial troubles. I was forced to deal with problems that I had previously covered up by treating myself to a favorite restaurant or going on a shopping spree. As a result, I began thinking more seriously about my life.

I anticipated that January 1, 2005 would not only mark my 22nd birthday, but also the start of a new, more positive and empowered me. I was dedicated to moving my life forward, graduating from college, starting law school, and relishing in a successful career as a highly sought after criminal defense attorney (the female Johnny Cochran!).

So that evening, instead of praying and asking for things I needed and wanted in my life, I chose to reflect on the progress I experienced as a whole. I began *praising and thanking* God for even the smallest of blessings. Then I began "exchanging who(s)" as Christian pastor Paula White calls it. It's when you tell God "who" He is in your life and He begins to tell you "who" you are in His Light.

In a flash, a vision opened up before me: There I was on a stage with a commanding presence. I had a microphone in my hand and I was speaking with pure passion and emotion. There was a huge crowd before me. I didn't know what I was saying in The Vision, but whatever it was, it had the crowd moved as well. The Vision was crystal clear. It was as if someone had flung me into the future, like the Ghost of Christmas Yet To Come, and I had the opportunity to watch myself in action years from now. I was a powerful woman. I looked good; I was healthy and vibrant, and completely in my element.

The Vision only lasted for a few moments before I snapped out of it. I quickly got off my knees and sat at the edge of my bed trying to make sense of what I just witnessed. Was the Vision foretelling that I was going to be a preacher? At first glance, that's what it looked like. I was speaking with the same passion and emotion that I witnessed with preachers. The crowd could have very well been a church congregation. I started to feel a little depressed at the thought of it all. I make a point to always be honest with myself and the truth of the matter was: I did not want to be a preacher! Even worse, when I went over all the details of The Vision in my mind, it was undeniably apparent to me that I was NOT an attorney. I was completely unnerved. All my life I had a sense of direction. I always had a plan and my plan had a plan.

If becoming an attorney was not a part of my future and preaching wasn't something I would pursue, then what now? As I sat at the edge of my bed searching for answers I came to this conclusion: Just disregard The Vision, continue studying for the LSAT (Law School Admissions Test) and it'll all just go away. But somehow in the coming days I couldn't shake the effects of the experience. When I studied for the LSAT, it just didn't feel right anymore. Two weeks went by before I prayed again, because I was afraid that I would see more of The Vision.

January 1, 2005 came and went and I settled into finishing my last year of college, and preparing for the next phase of my life. In March of that year, I was invited to a local church for a Women's Month career event. It was a great opportunity to network with professional, like-minded women. As I made my way around to each vendor, I stopped at a table presenting an opportunity to start your own financial services business. I spoke with the lady at the table, gave her my information for a follow-up call, and proceeded to the next booth.

At home that night, I carefully went over all the materials I picked up that day. When I came across the booklet for the financial services business I realized how much the thought of owning my own business allured me. In the past, I always chose positions that allowed me freedom and control of my time and income. At 18, I was selling Avon. At 20, I sold cutlery part time and enjoyed a paid position as a principal dancer with a traveling West African ensemble. I decided to give this new opportunity a try. *It felt right.* A few days after I made the decision, my Spirit quietly confirmed to me that in The Vision I was not a preacher...I was an entrepreneur. That's the only realization I was given at that point.

I believe that great things are found in the Spirit of positivity and praise. Expressing deep gratitude at the lowest times can and will transform your life. In an environment of gratitude, not only can you find your purpose, but you may also get a glimpse of what it looks like. It's also important to keep an open mind. Because I didn't know my heart's desire, I couldn't recognize it when I saw it. What The Vision entailed is what I've wanted all along.

> **"Expressing deep gratitude at the lowest times can and will transform your life."**

We have to apply patience and allow the plan to unfold. If you know you've received a Divine vision, it will surely come to pass. For the remainder of that year I embraced my destiny. The road wasn't always easy, but with every step, I gained clarity and confidence. After graduation, instead of applying to law school, I went head first into business, managing a fine arts company. Four years later, with lots of experience under my belt and a trail of proven, successes, I launched Queen of the South Motivational Speaking, Seminars & Consulting. I came to realize that in The Vision, I was not only an entrepreneur, but also a dynamic motivational speaker. The pieces to the puzzle were coming together, and they still are. Like I always say, as the vision gets nearer, it gets clearer.

33 Principles To A G.R.E.A.T. Life

Principle 3:
A G.R.E.A.T. person is a visionary.

Day 4

Taking Inventory

"Know thyself means this, that you get acquainted with what you know, and what you can do."

– Menander

"He that will not reflect is a ruined man."

– Asian Proverb

R eal success is built on a foundation of Truth. Whether you acknowledge it or not the Truth still exists. Your unwillingness to embrace it won't change the ultimate reality. One of the most powerful success secrets I know is to be true to yourself. If you want to experience the great life, you must be *honest* about your situation. Genuinely evaluate your life and know where you are and where you want to go.

Graduating from college was a pivotal point in my life. Not only because I was the first in my family to do so (on my

31

mom's side), but because reality began to sink in. All my life, I had these grand visions and dreams of what my future would be like. Now a college graduate, the real world was staring me in the face. I began to think to myself: What makes me different from others who've dreamed big dreams and found themselves years later empty-handed and settling for much, much less? I became increasingly aware that playtime was over.

I took a good, hard look at my situation. Four-and-a-half years prior, I left home for college in search of a better life in every aspect. I set out with the mindset to be different but December 13, 2005 (one day after graduation) found me sitting on my couch in a state of shock, realizing that the very things I was running from, I had run into. I was knee deep in credit card debt and other consumer loans. Growing up with limited resources, I decided when I went off to college that I would always have the best life had to offer. I was getting lots of money from scholarship overages; I had access to several credit cards and department store cards. I bought what I wanted when I wanted. I thought I had it all figured out. I did pay my bills on time, but a few setbacks totally collapsed the house of cards I built. Now, here I was in the same financial situation I experienced growing up.

Physically, I had been petite all my life, but due to lack of exercise in my last semester, I had 16 extra pounds on my small frame. With a family history of high blood pressure and diabetes, I knew the path I was heading towards. Professionally, I was proud of my Bachelors of Science in Criminology, but I had decided nine months before graduation that I wouldn't take the path of pursuing a law degree. Spiritually, I had so many questions about life. Honest questions that I just needed some answers to...

Sitting on that couch I felt my life was in complete disarray. Then a Voice from within whispered: "If you want something different you have to do something different. If you can change your thoughts, you can change your life." I immediately began to take inventory. I started by answering the questions: Where am I right now? Where do I want to be? I assessed every detail of my life and began to identify behaviors and habits that were not serving me. It's a common saying that change doesn't happen overnight. I disagree. There are times when profound change can happen in a second. It's the very definition of a defining moment. This was truly the day that my life changed forever, because I made a *decision*. A mental shift occurred. I began to see things in a new light. I embraced Truth and added right action. It's the formula that led me to where I am today and it's the formula that will take me further up the ladder of greatness.

"If you are ready to go to the next level, it's time to do some serious evaluation."

If you are ready to go to the next level, it's time to do some serious evaluation. Write down all your strengths and areas of opportunity. Know the things that are working for your good and be willing to admit the things that aren't. If it's not working, get rid of it. Like dead foliage on a plant, the ineffective parts of your life are stunting you growth. Prune what you can to produce the best results.

After you've taken an honest, naked look at yourself, take a long, deep breath and be thankful. Whether good or bad, you should feel extreme gratitude for having an awareness of where you are in your life because awareness is power. All of your life experiences have led you to this point. This is the beginning of the next level on your journey to greatness. You are in a position to finally experience all that the Universe has to offer.

As I said on Day 3, great things are found in the Spirit of positivity, gratitude, and praise. If you truly believe that you are called to greatness, get excited. You may be knee-deep in debt, physically unhealthy, and unfocused in your mind, but all that can change in an instant. Remember, a spiritual and mental shift precedes material change. When you start thinking differently, you'll act differently, and your life will transform. Never mind what the past looks like; you are about to transcend to another level spiritually and mentally that will produce better days starting NOW (Job 8:7).

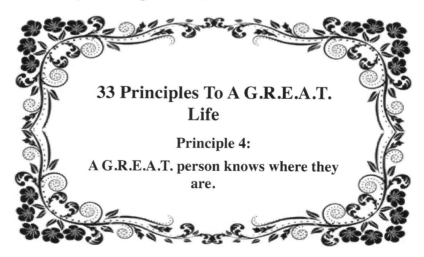

33 Principles To A G.R.E.A.T. Life

Principle 4:

A G.R.E.A.T. person knows where they are.

Day 5

Accepting Change

"We are all called, but few accept the challenge of a calling. Why? Because accepting your calling will change your life."

– Terrie Williams

"No one can follow it down through the ages without realizing that the whole purpose of existence is GROWTH. Life is dynamic—not static. It is ever moving forward—not standing still."

– Robert Collier

After you've taken stock of yourself, you will find that in order to get where you want to go some radical changes are required. We have all heard the saying that "the only thing constant in life is change." As we look around our lives, we can agree that this is true. Our world is ever changing, always moving. The Earth is moving right now, so fast that you think you're standing still.

So if change is an inevitable, natural part of life, why do we resist it? One reason is that we become emotionally attached to things, people, and circumstances. We create soul ties that are hard to break. Fear is another factor in resisting change. It is very common to fear the unknown, and change can surely be uncertain. Complacency is also a reason. For some, the status quo may not be the best situation, but like your favorite warm, worn-out blanket it is familiar and comfortable. Whatever the reason, resisting change and being stuck in our ways can stunt our growth.

Embracing change is important to living a great life. But in order to accept it, we must understand it. As we become aware of the true nature

> "Embracing change is important to living a great life."

of change, we begin to develop a more positive perception of it. I always say that the Siamese twin of change is growth. It's impossible to grow without some form of *transformation*. To live is to progress and move forward, so if there's nothing to challenge you to keep growing, then you've stopped living. Stand still and resist change and you will be swept away by the flow of life.

Sometimes in order to move to the next level, we need to learn a new skill set or step outside of ourselves and accept a new method of doing things. A good example is the computer age. As the use of personal computers grew in the 1990s and into the new millennium, Generation Y embraced the changes as older generations grew resistant to this new technology. Most of our parents and grandparents didn't want to be bothered with the Internet, complicated cell phones, e-mails, or social networking sites. These same people, especially those in business, now realize that in order to function in this age, they have to have at least a basic understanding of modern technology. They have to get with the program, or as I like to say, *move with the movement*.

Change is a two-sided coin. On one side is the end of a thing and on the other side there are new beginnings. Your perception will determine whether the change is good or bad. However, a great person knows that change, even when it's most difficult, always brings a greater reward.

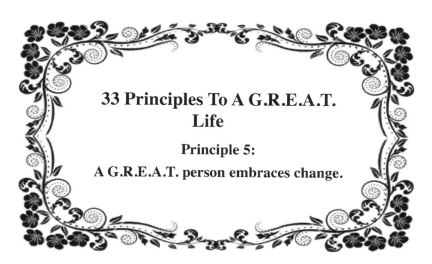

33 Principles To A G.R.E.A.T. Life

Principle 5:

A G.R.E.A.T. person embraces change.

Day 6

I Just Wanted to Fly

"If you surrender to the wind, you can ride it."
– Toni Morrison

"Come to the edge, He said.
They said, we are afraid.
Come to the edge, He said.
They came.
He pushed them…and they flew."

– Guillaume Apollinaire

Have you ever felt like you just wanted to break free, spread your wings, and fly? I feel at some point in life, we all do. It's a natural human urge to want to soar to higher heights and be in an environment where we can experience complete freedom. As acclaimed author and spiritual teacher Iyanla Vanzant said, "We are all *built* to fly." Yes, it's true, we are all built to fly…but it doesn't mean we ever will. To have the potential to do a thing is never enough. In order to fly, you have to be aware that you can then, you have to test your wings.

On your journey to greatness, it's important to have an environment that encourages you to explore the height of your potential. You need to be in a position where you can *thrive*. Unfortunately, there are times when external factors constrict our creativity and growth. Being held in a certain mold because of the past can make it difficult to grow in our environment. I can recall times when I wanted to soar higher, but I could not crack the shell of expectations that others placed on me due to past experiences.

> "On your journey to greatness, it's important to have an environment that encourages you to explore the height of your potential."

On one such occasion, I was sitting at my kitchen table staring at my Peace Lily. I suddenly realized that my plant and I had a lot in common. The Lily was a gift from over a year ago. It was a much smaller plant then, so I placed it in a vase that fit, but still gave it room to grow. Over the year, with water, sunlight, and pruning, the Peace Lily grew tremendously. I realized months ago that it was time to put the Lily in a bigger vase where it could continue to blossom with ease. Instead, I procrastinated and now I was staring at a plant that looked extremely uncomfortable. There appeared to be a thousand roots at the bottom of the glass vase. Like me, my Lily had so much potential for growth, but it was being restricted by its environment. I decided right then that in order to break free I had to create a space where I could fully embrace myself regardless of the criticism or negative energy thrown my way.

In African folklore there are stories of a tribe that could literally fly. It is said that the "Spanish stopped importing them as slaves because so many of them flew away that it was bad for business." Singing in their native tongue, they would stretch their hands and fly away home to Africa. They could not bear the burden of being slaves. Like these people, I could never tolerate living beneath my potential. At a very early age I realized that a dead end life was not for me. I had to release old, ineffective beliefs and traditions that were weighing me down and throwing dirt on my wings.

> **"No matter how restricted we may become in our circumstances, there's always something in us that wants to be free."**

I had to break free and go to a new place that somehow felt strangely familiar. I was finding my way home.

No matter how restricted we may become in our circumstances, there's always something in us that wants to be free. Don't settle for low-level living. Explore the possibility of who you can be and what you can do if you

40

"surrender to the wind." Heed the higher calling of your Spirit and venture to the edge. It's time to test your wings and discover that you can fly.

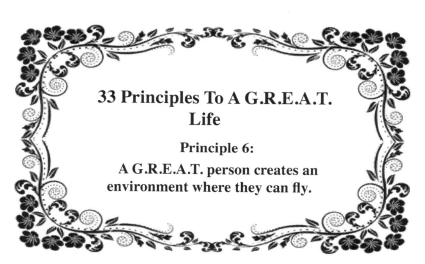

33 Principles To A G.R.E.A.T. Life

Principle 6:

A G.R.E.A.T. person creates an environment where they can fly.

Day 7

Get Organized

"I make it a rule to clear my desk every day, before leaving my office, of all correspondence and memoranda, so that on the morrow I can begin a new day of work."

– Booker T. Washington

"Write the vision, make it plain."

– Habakkuk 2:2

Organization is a Divine pursuit. Like many things in life it requires consistent effort. If we want to transcend from good to great, we have to be clear about what we want and make definite decisions to reach our goals. When our thoughts and actions are scattered, unclear, and unfocused, we experience stagnation, lack of motivation, lethargy and even depression. Unorganized efforts produce a weak aim that may or may not reach the target. But clear thinking and concentration is power, and power applied to goals equal success.

42

Organization will make your dreams a reality. Success comes in knowing how to align your gifts and talents in a way that makes sense. I had to learn this strategy the hard way. I spent two years of my life trying to pursue all of my dreams at once. I ended up getting little accomplished. I can admit that I'm a chronic multi-tasker, so instead of pursuing 10 goals at a time, I picked the two or three things that I was most passionate about and started there.

Realize that spreading yourself thin is an energy zapper. You don't have to do it all now. Instead, identify the activities that you should pursue immediately from the ones that you can start a little later. Then commit to setting clearly defined goals. Instead of using vague and broad terms, get specific and lay out every detail. Write it all down; make it plain. When you do this, your dreams can manifest at the speed of light.

Just as important as organizing your thoughts, goals, and dreams is organizing your workspace and living environment. In order to receive the greater things in life, we have to make room for them by letting go of some good things. In other words: *Clear the clutter!* I have been so guilty of this. I had to stretch myself to become neater in my workspace, my home, and my car. All of my surroundings were in constant disarray. My rationale was that as long as I knew where everything was, it was okay. As I began to grow in awareness, I ditched the "organized chaos" theory. A cluttered mess simply does not support a great lifestyle.

When you walk into a room that is organized and neat, you immediately get a positive vibration. If this room is your workspace, you feel motivated to be effective and get things done. On the other hand, you can be in the best of moods and walk into a cluttered, stuffy room and it can zap your energy. A positive attitude is so important on this journey, so do your best to create a fresh perspective and fresh energy when starting each day. Remember your physical surroundings are a projection of your inner activity. If I compared myself now to where I was 1 year ago, I'm proud to say that I'm doing *a lot* better in keeping my spaces neater. I now recognize organization as a tool to achieve and maintain a great life.

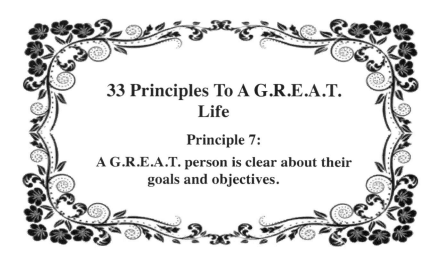

33 Principles To A G.R.E.A.T. Life

Principle 7:

A G.R.E.A.T. person is clear about their goals and objectives.

PART II:

Be Resilient

From Good to G.R.E.A.T.

Day 8

University of Adversity

"When you come to the end of your rope, tie a knot and hang on."

– Franklin D. Roosevelt

"Many of life's failures are people who did not realize how close they were to success when they gave up."

– Thomas Edison

"Realize that you may encounter many defeats but you must not be defeated. It may even be necessary to encounter the defeats, so you can know who you are, how you can rely upon yourself, and where you can pull yourself up from."

– Maya Angelou

The ability to bounce back from adversity is a characteristic of every successful leader and great individual. We call it *resilience*. In part one, we've established that we all have a purpose and a higher calling, but the best in you will emerge through the training grounds of adversity. I've met influential people who have impressive degrees from the most prestigious academic institutions in the country, but a traditional education does not ensure greatness. Although I have a Bachelors degree from a great college, the degree that means the most to me is the one I earned at the University of Adversity in the School of Hard Knocks. It's a G.R.E.A.T. institution of *higher* learning.

"At the University of Adversity, the tuition may be steep, but the rewards are great."

So you want to live the great life, but have you added the cost? Some people don't consider that there might be a cost, so when the bill arrives they run, hide and eventually default. So I'll ask you again, now that you've stepped onto the road to greatness, have you considered the cost? What price are you willing to pay to live your dreams? Many times the cost won't be in dollar form; you may have to pay in sweat equity, faith and perseverance.

At the University of Adversity, the tuition may be steep, but the rewards are great. If you will only keep going and don't quit you will reach your destination and not only enjoy the great life, but also have the depth of character to handle the success. We've all heard the horror stories of people who win the lottery but didn't have the character to use the new fortune wisely. These people ended up worse off than they were before. Great success that hasn't been molded on the wheel of adversity is like a 40-foot skyscraper with no foundation. It's a dangerous thing and when it falls, it falls hard and loud.

I've been in some low places in my life: not enough money, not enough food. Many times I was left empty-handed with nothing but big dreams and a Spirit that wouldn't let me quit. As motivational speaker Les Brown says, "In your prosperous times you put it in your pocket. In your lean times you put in your heart." I had to learn how to make my pain count. I began to focus on the lessons in each situation to move forward. There were times when I couldn't run to the finish line, I had to walk. And even worse times when I couldn't walk, I had to crawl. And then the really low times when I couldn't crawl; all I could do was wiggle just to let Life know I was still in the game. I refused to be defeated.

"Great individuals are like spiritual bodybuilders. They eat challenges for breakfast!"

I realized that the weight of adversity should only make us stronger. Without challenges, we would be spiritual pipsqueaks. Great individuals are like spiritual bodybuilders. They eat challenges for breakfast! It's not to say that their challenges are easier, but we are designed to overcome adversity, and any great person knows that.

Every day, life presents us with obstacles that provide

opportunities for growth in order to move to a higher level. Now that I finally *realize* this, when I encounter heavy situations I get excited knowing that on the other side of this challenge is the success I've been yearning for. There's so much more I want out of life and I believe the best is yet to come. Although I'm proud of my work at the University of Adversity, I don't plan to stop there. I recently enrolled in the graduate program!

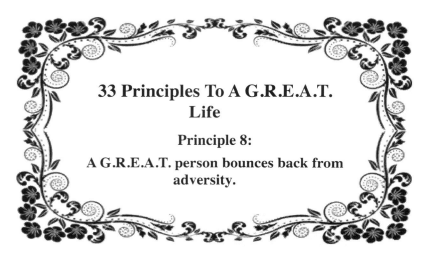

33 Principles To A G.R.E.A.T. Life

Principle 8:

A G.R.E.A.T. person bounces back from adversity.

Day 9

The Heart of Darkness

"You need chaos in your soul to give birth to a dancing star."

– Nietzsche

"I've learned that you can tell a lot about a person by the way (s)he handles a rainy day."

– Maya Angelou

"Every adversity, every failure, every heartache carries with it the seed of an equivalent success."

– Napoleon Hill

A re you afraid of the dark? I used to be until I began to understand the duality of its nature. Most people perceive darkness as a negative concept, but great things can emerge from darkness. According to Genesis 1:2, the world as we know it came forth from a blue black, formless substance. The darkest color, black, holds every conceivable color known to man. No other color in the Universe has that potential. In that way, the darkness holds every conceivable possibility. On the positive end of the spectrum, darkness represents raw, untapped potential.

The bigger the dream you have, a deeper foundation must be laid. You may be working underground for years before you get to start on level one. On the other hand, you may reach your goal in a relatively short period of time, and the deep foundation may pertain to your experiences. When we encounter profound hardship it deepens our character and instantly gives us a new outlook on life.

In many cases, the most essential parts of a creation grow in a place we can't see. A tree stands solid and strong because the roots underground are deep and strong. Valuable natural resources are found underground or in dark mines. A baby develops into a human being inside the comforting darkness of its mother's womb. Babies are so used to a darker environment that sometimes it takes days before they are able to open their eyes for a sustained period of time.

I realized that underground, in the trenches, is where you build the best character. It's in the dark smoldering embers, just when you thought it was over, that the phoenix rises from the ashes and experiences a radical transformation and *rebirth*. It's in the dark incubating cocoon that the caterpillar realizes its greatest potential and breaks free as a butterfly.

We couldn't appreciate light if it were not for darkness. As a matter of fact, we couldn't appreciate life if it wasn't for darkness. Dark, cloudy days bring rain, and rain is necessary to sustain life and for new life to emerge. In the dark hours between late night and early morning we take our rest. Holistic health experts refer to sleep as an eight-hour healing session because, at that time our bodies are repairing damage and rejuvenating itself for another day.

Many times on this journey to greatness, you'll have to go into a dark place. Know that this time is necessary. Skipping steps in these dark times can lead to cracks in your foundation. No matter how big a life you build on a cracked foundation, eventually you will have to go back to the beginning to restructure or worse, tear everything down and start all over. Take this time to rejuvenate and build your character. Although dark, this period in your life doesn't have to be a negative one. When you're living a great life, you can find a positive element in all things. Every moment becomes a teachable moment as you climb the ladder of excellence.

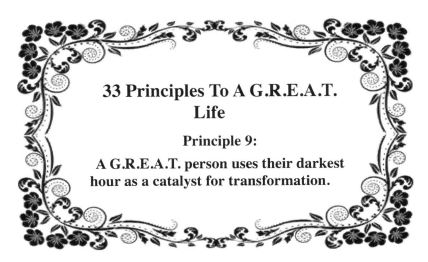

33 Principles To A G.R.E.A.T. Life

Principle 9:

A G.R.E.A.T. person uses their darkest hour as a catalyst for transformation.

Day 10

God Is in the Character-Building Business

"Consider it a sheer gift, friends, when tests and challenges come at you from all sides. You know that under pressure, your faith-life is forced into the open and shows its true colors. So don't try to get out of anything prematurely. Let it do its work so you become mature and well-developed, not deficient in any way."

– James 2:4 (The Message Bible)

"I know God will not give me anything I can't handle. I just wish that He didn't trust me so much."

– Mother Teresa

"Potentially, man is stronger than his fears and greater than his weaknesses."

– Eric Butterworth

Our Universe is a place of opulence and abundance. We have the ability to receive the best in life in unlimited quantities. If this is true, then why are so many of us living in lack? Would it not be a good thing for you to have the material success you want: that business, house, car, or great relationship? It would be... when you're ready for it. It's only through character building that we can achieve everything we desire; and it is best this way. Receive any "good thing" prematurely and it could destroy you.

Perception of adversity is truly what separates the good from the great. Great people don't mind being in the trenches and doing the work it takes to build character in order to advance to the next level. Unfortunately, many people would rather have a glass of water conveniently handed to them than have the directions to the Well where the water flows from an unlimited Source. Why? Because the walk is too long, the sun is too hot, and the road is uncertain. There are twists and turns, steep parts and jagged areas. But if they would just take up the task, they would never thirst again.

How many times do we ask for great things not realizing that the way is through the Refiner's fire? The minute we feel the heat we jump out of the pot not allowing the work in us to be completed. When gold is refined all the impurities bubble to the surface leaving a pure product.

The process can be ugly, but the outcome is pure gold of the highest value. Pure gold represents a heightened spiritual consciousness, and we all should strive for it. Literally, pure gold is expensive, but try buying it spiritually from the Supplier himself! (Revelations 3:18).

A great person once said, "Failure inspires winners and defeats losers." So which are you? When I was 5 years old, my mother placed me in my first beauty pageant competition. I walked away with the crown and the title of "Miss Cumberland Preschool 1988." 11 years later in 1999 and at the age of 16, I competed in my second pageant and won that title as well. Over the course of 10 years (1999-2009) I competed in 40 oratorical and pageant competition. I held a record of 19 wins, and secured a runner-up spot in every pageant but three. To me, winning was taking home the crown; and that was my only goal. I never gave any energy to being Miss Congeniality or selling the most ads, I went for the gusto!

> "Pure gold represents a heightened spiritual consciousness, and we all should strive for it."

The year 2003 was a fantastic time for me in pageantry. By the middle of the year, I was on a six-pageant winning streak. This success came with mixed emotions. On one hand, I was exhilarated. I was confident and on top of my game. I may have become a little too confident! But on the other hand, I had become extremely self-conscious. I felt I had hit a high plateau with nowhere else to go but down.

The seventh pageant that year was a regional-level college fraternity competition held in Hilton Head, South Carolina. I was excited and scared at the same time. I loved pageantry, but expectations were high and I wasn't feeling up to par. I became so self-conscious about what others expected of me and the fact that the winning streak would have to end someday, that on the morning of the pageant I completely bombed personal interviews.

That night, I was announced first runner up in the competition. I was completely unnerved. Deep down I knew that my low interview score was what hurt me, but the situation still bothered me. I was *supposed* to win... in my mind. I called friends, telling the story to try to get support that I must've been cheated. Leaving Hilton Head the next day, I called my dad and talked to him about the pageant. His reply was: "How do you expect to grow if you're getting crowned every time?"

I got the message then and walked away from that experience with a new definition of a winner. True winners grow from every experience whether good or bad. In pageantry, winners may not go home with the crown, but by allowing the experience to be an avenue for personal development they receive much more than a shiny tiara. That's just the icing on the cake. Sometimes in order to grow we must fail. If things are always going our way, how can we develop the character to receive greater things? After that experience, I went on to do more pageants, getting the crown on some or just a runner-up place, but I won them all.

In the last pageant of my career, I was asked in my interview competition, "If you don't win tonight, will it change anything?" I confidently answered, "Although I would love to be crowned Miss Black USA, the character that I've developed in preparing for this pageant is my greatest reward." I really meant it. When we allow our experiences to birth strong character and we use that character to move forward, we are successful.

There's always something to work on and there's always room to grow. We are our own life's project. God sees ahead and knows what character we need to develop to receive great things. Yes, it may hurt sometimes, but as my friend and mastermind partner Lori Pelzer says, "Would we be extraordinary if it was easy?" I know the fire is hot, but if you persevere, a new you will emerge. So learn your lessons and keep on climbing. The great life awaits you.

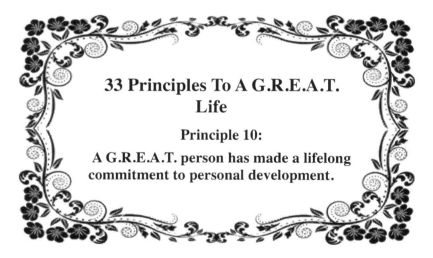

33 Principles To A G.R.E.A.T. Life

Principle 10:

A G.R.E.A.T. person has made a lifelong commitment to personal development.

Day 11

Growing Pains

"Anyone who has never made a mistake has never tried anything new."

– Albert Einstein

"Welcome all experiences. You never know which one is going to turn everything on."

– Jim Rohn

"Success in life is the result of good judgment. Good judgment is usually the result of experience. Experience is usually the result of bad judgment."

– Anthony Robbins

We are living in a time when the use of painkillers is at epidemic proportions. People are being medicated for any and everything. The reality is we would rather be drugged up than face the real issues in our lives. We are eager to medicate the symptoms instead of dealing directly with the problem. And what's worse, many of these medications can cause more serious side effects than the problem itself. Taking depression drugs may cause insomnia, fatigue, urinary difficulties, sexual dysfunction, vomiting, suicidal thoughts, and even death. Whoa, as if a clinically depressed person doesn't have enough problems! There are severe cases when a person should be medicated, but if you're feeling depressed, instead of only masking your problem with medication, look for the purpose in the pain. Sometimes God uses pain as a way to get your attention and get you back on track. You'll never move pass the pain to a better place by covering it up.

Pain is just another opportunity for growth, hence the term: growing pains. This can be an excellent time for self-discovery. Often the origin of the pain is tucked away and buried in an obscure place within us. It may be as difficult to find as the proverbial needle in the haystack.

In an episode of one of my favorite television shows,

> "Pain is just another opportunity for growth, hence the term: growing pains. This can be an excellent time for self-discovery."

House, there was a young girl who was experiencing failure of her vital organs. The girl was dying fast and no one knew why. They tested her for every possible disease they could think of. As his patient lay dying, House suddenly remembered that poisoning from a tick could cause the violent reactions. He examined her body and found the tick on the inside of her leg where it could have been easily overlooked. He pulled it away and the girl immediately began to recover. A teeny-tiny insect was the cause of so much damage.

To get over the pain, we may just need a slight adjustment in our attitude or outlook on life. When we deal with pain head on and work through our issues, our health is restored and our lives return to normal.

> "When we deal with pain head on and work through our issues, our health is restored and our lives return to normal."

I've been in uncomfortable situations where the pain was so bad that I thought it would never go away. I could see no light at the end of the tunnel, but I rested in the fact that any hurt can be healed.

It's a common saying that "things that are covered do not heal well." Instead of running away and resisting the pain, find a place where you can expose the injury and accelerate the restoration process. I have learned that a major sign of spiritual maturity is being willing to accept the painful lessons of life without stubbornness and resistance.

As we covered in Part 1, a great life is lived in purpose and passion. It's important that you operate in Divine purpose because in those times when obstacles get in your way and the pain seems unbearable, passion can be the impetus that gets you thru the pain. Whether the pain is prolonged or short lived, your deepest desires remind you why you must overcome and what you have to look forward to when this season passes. Don't do yourself the disservice of covering up the pain. Keep pushing. It always gets better.

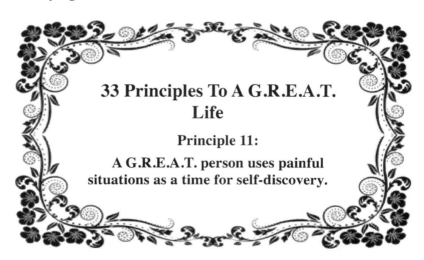

33 Principles To A G.R.E.A.T. Life

Principle 11:

A G.R.E.A.T. person uses painful situations as a time for self-discovery.

Day 12

What Do *You* Think?

"You can do as much as you think you can,
But you'll never accomplish more;
If you're afraid of yourself, young man,
There's little for you in store.
For failure comes from the inside first,
It's there if we only knew it,
And you can win, though you face the worst,
If you feel that you're going to do it."

– Edgar A. Guest

"There's a lot of water out in the ocean, but it
can't sink your ship unless it gets inside."

– Dick Gregory

"If you're firmly rooted in the ground, you're not
so easily pushed over."

– Maya Angelou

In order to break through to the great life, you have to have a fortified mind and iron clad faith. When you're sure of your vision, and you set your feet in the right direction, you have to learn how to deflect the negative comments and attitudes of others. You must not allow negativity or ignorance to sow weeds of doubt in your faith garden. By ignorance, I mean not knowing, lacking knowledge. When you're on a Divine path, no one can see the vision the way you can. We should always be open to constructive criticism, but keep in mind that those who lack information of your plans or dreams should not have the final say on your actions.

Building the foundation of your vision requires intense focus and concentration, so it's important to continue seeking the kingdom within. When you stay connected, it's easier to discern constructive criticism from destructive criticism, or opportunities that will advance you along your path from opportunities that will take you away from your goal.

There are times in our lives when we have to leave something really good to pursue something great. I've heard countless stories of people who earned six-figure incomes leaving their corporate jobs to pursue their dreams. Amidst heavy criticism from family, friends, and colleagues they accepted less money while pursuing their heart's desire. These individuals knew that the security of their former job was just an illusion. Being unfulfilled in a high-stress, high-paying job is not the key to living. When these brave souls made that huge leap they were after something greater. They could not allow the short-sighted opinions of others to thwart their plans. They understood that if they could just believe in themselves and forge ahead, eventually they would have not only a lucrative career, but also a fulfilled life and a peaceful existence.

When I made the decision to switch career paths and go into business, many people thought that I was making a HUGE mistake. To make matters worse, I decided to go into business with my boyfriend of only three months. You can just imagine what people had to say! According to others, this man had obviously derailed my dreams. I had this great future as an attorney and now I was throwing it all away for a guy I just met. Likely story, but I saw The Vision, and that was enough for me. Because I saw the plan, I was able to spot opportunity where others could not. Partnering with my beau proved to be one of the best decisions I have ever made. You have to take responsibility for the things in your life that you did or didn't do. You only get one life to live, why waste it living according to what others think.

> "You only get one life to live; why waste it living according to what others think."

Stay with the vision, because the end will speak. There are many people in life who could have accomplished great things, but they allowed the opinions of others to kill their creativity. John Eliot said, "History shows us that the people who end up changing the world – the great political, social, scientific, technological, artistic, even sports revolutionaries – are always nuts, until they are right, and then they are geniuses." Others may tell you something is impossible because it is impossible to *them*. However, you control what you let enter your mind and heart. What matters the most is what you think of yourself.

In 2008 when the economy was on a steep decline, I had to make a serious decision for my life and career as an entrepreneur. I had just opened an online clothing store and my business was steady despite the economy, but I wanted to expand. After restructuring my finances, I knew that I would need to supplement my income somehow. I didn't need much, and after giving it some thought, I decided that a waitressing job would be the best fit for me. I could enjoy shorter work hours and cash every day. I needed that flexibility and a steady supply of cash to invest in the business.

I chose an upscale restaurant about two miles away from my home. I got the job on the spot which was a positive sign for me. Then reality hit me: here I am, a college graduate working as a waitress! But I threw that to the back of my mind. I was on a mission. For the nine months I was there, I kept my job to myself and a few people who could understand my path. All my life I had been able to overcome obstacles and achieve at higher levels. Many people who were used to me as the "high-achiever" would not be able to understand this move. I simply could not afford the distraction of their criticism. I saw my goal; I had to focus. I began to realize that in order to have success you must know what success looks like. Success is not the big house, big car, and the big bank account. Success is that young woman working double time to fund her dreams. Success is that young man who rides a bike to a 10-hour job, then comes home and stays up late working on his vision.

The time may come when even those closest to you will lose faith in your abilities. All the talk of one day making it big becomes just "talk" to them. If you want to live the great life, you must master the art of encouraging yourself. When the going gets tough, the great keep going. Why? Because they understand that "no one is ever defeated until defeat has been accepted as a reality." (Napoleon Hill)

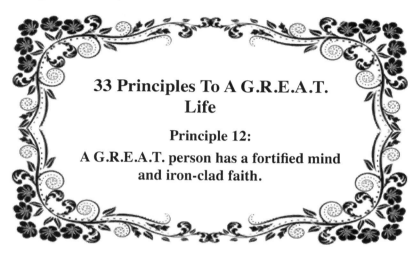

33 Principles To A G.R.E.A.T. Life

Principle 12:

A G.R.E.A.T. person has a fortified mind and iron-clad faith.

Day 13

Creative Vision

"Capital isn't scarce; vision is."

– Sam Walton

"The man who says it cannot be done should not interrupt the man doing it."

– Chinese Proverb

"Don't let anyone rob you of your imagination, your creativity, or your curiosity. It's your place in the world; it's your life. Go on and do all you can with it, and make it the life you want to live."

– Mae Jemison

If you want something greater, you have to position yourself for it. You have to have the ability to see things on a different level. This requires an open mind and creative vision. We must look beyond the surface and believe in the unfolding potential of everything, including ourselves. It's not about who you are now but who you *can* become.

Most people would declare that they are not creative. About five years ago I was one in that bunch. I would observe people who I thought were extremely creative and watch as they would easily come up with great ideas. I resigned myself to the fact that I just wasn't born with a lot of creativity. When I began to understand the natural laws of the Universe I realized that the way to become more creative is to use the little creativity that I have and push it to the limits. I've been using this method ever since. Now great ideas come to me so fast and so often that I have to keep a voice recorder nearby at all times! *I am a creative person whose creativity grows more and more every day.* And anyone should believe the same of themselves. We have, within us, access to unlimited creativity that we can pull on and use anytime we want. It's only when we rely on the outside world that we experience limitations.

Napoleon Hill teaches that "the starting point of all achievement is desire," because desire and passion forces creativity. When you mix passion with creativity you will always find a way to meet any goal. Forget what you heard. There's always a way. The Almighty wouldn't put you in a situation where there's no hope. Just look around to find the ram in the bush. When you genuinely believe that anything is possible, you will receive Divine ideas that will direct you towards your goal.

I'm in support of formal education, but sometimes when we pursue things in a structured environment it kills our creativity. To unleash your creativity, you have to break out of your self-imposed barriers. You must begin to think outside the box. Despite what we were taught in preschool, it's okay to color outside the lines. The world would be a boring place without the fresh air of innovation.

Creativity is an essential tool on the journey to greatness. Especially if you are starting your journey with limited resources, you may have to use unconventional means to reach your goal. There are times when I find myself in situations where my back is against the wall and I only have two options: get it done or get it done. Instead of panicking, I open my mind and search for what I have in my immediate possession because I know that there is a solution to every problem. *It's Universal law*. When we take our abilities and push them to the limit, then wrap them in Divine power, we become unstoppable.

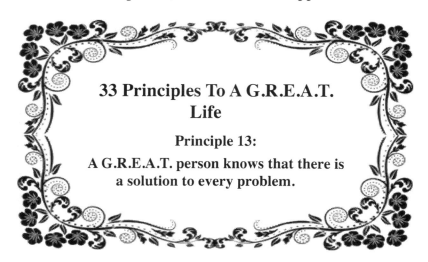

33 Principles To A G.R.E.A.T. Life

Principle 13:
A G.R.E.A.T. person knows that there is a solution to every problem.

Day 14

A Cure For Stagnation

"We can't solve problems by using the same kind of thinking we used when we created them."

– Albert Einstein

We all have encountered periods of stagnation in our lives. Whether from negativity, lack of awareness, or intimidation of an obstacle, there are times when we find ourselves lacking the energy to move forward. For instance, an adverse situation comes your way and instead of focusing on your goals you find yourselves festering in negative stew. Or maybe that hectic schedule has you blowing like a leaf in the wind and you're not mindful of the present moment. Living with a lack of awareness is like living in a trance state. You may go for months even years in stagnation before you awake from sleep walking through life. Then there are times when you find yourself on the right track, but the next obstacle to overcome seems so big that you become intimidated and overwhelmed. Fear sets in and you are unable to take the first step.

I've learned that one cure for stagnation is to take immediate action BUT do things differently. It's really important to shake up the monotony and breathe new and fresh energy into our lives. When I find myself getting in a rut, I immediately switch things up. Believe it or not, sometimes it helps to rearrange the furniture in a room or open up a window and let some fresh air in. Maybe you need a change of scenery. If you are used to working on your goals in your office, take your work to the park instead or maybe just the front porch.

No matter how small, do something different. A refreshing change can create a more positive mood and clearer perception. On one occasion, I came home after a long day of running errands and attending meetings completely drained with a lot more work to do. It was a beautiful summer day but I was feeling sluggish, tired, and restless. Instead of entering my home from the front door, I decided to switch up the pace and go through the back door.

As I was walking through my backyard towards the patio, I stopped dead in my tracks. I looked around at the beautiful woodsy scenery and realized that I had not been in my own back yard for weeks. I forgot how beautiful and therapeutic it was. My hectic schedule had me running in circles, but the rejuvenation I needed was right under my nose. Instead of continuing up the steps, I sat down on my patio chair and took in the view. Then I closed my eyes, took a few deep breaths, and enjoyed the sounds of nature. I sat there for 30 minutes or so in peace and solitude.

When I opened my back door to go inside I was reinvigorated. My mind was clear and focused. With a renewed sense of direction, I went upstairs to my office and finished my work that day, but in a better mood and with more purpose and awareness. Previously, the mound of work on my desk had me stuck in inaction and indecision, but after that much needed break, I was able to clearly determine what needed to be done, and I resolved to do a little every day until the work was completed.

It's important to find a way to keep moving forward even during periods of frustration. In stagnant times, instead of focusing on taking 10 steps I focus on taking one step 10 times. Progress is progress. Reaching any goal creates a positive force you can build on. As the old adage goes, "If at first you don't succeed, try, try again." In other words, when you find yourself in a period of stagnation don't fret over wasted time. Take a break, do something different, hit the reset button and finish strong!

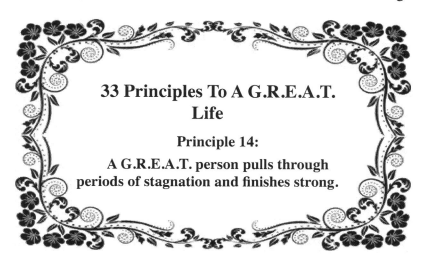

33 Principles To A G.R.E.A.T. Life

Principle 14:

A G.R.E.A.T. person pulls through periods of stagnation and finishes strong.

Day 15

Don't Forget to Be Thankful

"A pessimist sees the difficulty in every opportunity; an optimist sees the opportunity in every difficulty."

– Winston Churchill

"The grateful mind is constantly fixed upon the highest best; therefore it tends to become the best. Taking the form or character of the best, it will receive the best."

– Wallace D. Wattles

We have all heard the saying, "count your blessings." Well it's true. At all times we should be grateful, but even more so in times of adversity. Resist the urge to feel regret about where you are right now in your life. No matter what, it's all good!

Indeed, all things work together for good for those who heed the call of purpose (Romans 8:28). Every situation or experience is a pathway to the Divine.

Gratitude in the face of rough situations produces excellence and consistency of character. You cannot live a great life without these traits. It's easy to be positive in happy times, but maintaining great character in the midst of adversity will propel you to another level. Our Spirit is always looking for avenues to do powerful things. Great inventions, ideas, and inspiration are given to those who are open, genuine, and in a state of positivity. By constantly expressing gratitude we are transformed into a channel for greatness.

Whether in good or bad times, I wake up every morning giving thanks for a new day and acknowledging that everything I need to successfully complete this day has been given to me. I remember that I have been Divinely gifted with the power to overcome any obstacles in my path, and I assert that I am a magnet for great opportunities. As a result, every day I am discovering the keys to the kingdom and entering into the realm of abundance and life without limits.

The next time you attempt and fail, instead of focusing on the failure, realize that you may not have found what works, but at least you know one thing that doesn't. Although a failure, your efforts put you closer to uncovering the steps to realizing your dreams. Sometimes, I play a little game with myself. For every negative situation I encounter, I have to identify 3 things that are good about it. When we only focus on the negative things in life we create a blockage and great opportunities are denied to us. We can get so caught up in our own problems that we destroy the solutions. Don't allow life to rough you up so badly that you become spiritually constipated. As hilarious as it may sound, gratitude can work as a spiritual laxative that allows us to release the negative waste and toxins on the inside.

Remember, how you view failure and adversity determines greatness. Now that you realize that adversity is just a stepping stone to the next level, you can rest easy when challenges come your way. You understand that the obstacle is not to destroy you, but to develop you into the person you were always meant to be. Be thankful for these experiences and persevere. Soon, you'll find that you are no longer chasing your dreams. Your dreams are chasing you.

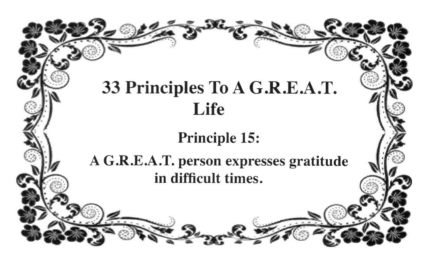

33 Principles To A G.R.E.A.T. Life

Principle 15:

A G.R.E.A.T. person expresses gratitude in difficult times.

PART III:

Be Empowered

Day 16

Follow The Yellow Brick Road

"We are not human beings having a spiritual experience, but spiritual beings having a human experience."

– Teilhard de Chardin

"But the greatest mistake is in believing that we are 'only human'…we are human in expression but divine in creation and limitless in potentiality."

– Eric Butterworth

"The kingdom of heaven is within you; and whosoever shall know himself shall find it."

– Ancient Egyptian Proverb

Who do you think you are? You may say, I am (insert name here), or I am a mother/father, a wife/husband, a business owner, a student, etc. However, the true essence of who you are has nothing to do with your name, your role, or your titles. That's all secondary and superficial. The Truth is you are a spiritual being with immense potential and unlimited power. I made the great discovery when I realized that there was more to me than skin and bones: I am a spiritual being *first*.

The purpose of the journeys in our lives is to grow and transcend the burdens that come with the human experience to become closer to our natural essence of Light. If we all could realize this fact, the world would be radically transformed in a blink of an eye. Exploring the concept of our unlimited power is an endless pursuit. To that effect, a great life is a rigorous course in self-discovery.

"The purpose of the journeys in our lives is to grow and transcend the burdens that come with the human experience to become closer to our natural essence of Light."

The Ancient Egyptians produced, arguably, the greatest civilization known to man. Largely because they lived by the creed: Know Thyself. Thousands of years before it appeared at the Greek Temple of Apollo at Delphi, "Know

Thyself" was inscribed on the walls of the pyramids. To many, this inscription means to know your history. This is important as well, but the Egyptians meant: know your inner self, your true nature. They believed that we can do the absolute impossible by way of Divine power that lives within each and every one of us. If this great civilization taught us anything it's that true genius can only be birthed from a spiritual realm. It's the reason why the pyramids are so hard to duplicate. The design for the structure was a Divine idea. Great and ingenious ideas are on a higher vibration and you must be spiritually and mentally elevated to receive them.

> "Great and ingenious ideas are on a higher vibration and you must be spiritually and mentally elevated to receive them."

Self-knowledge is truly the key to manifesting unlimited power. Now that you've committed yourself to personal development, you will experience new inner discoveries every day. There are moments of revelation and enlightenment all along this path. All you have to do is just *follow the yellow brick road*. Follow the clues and signs and allow them to lead the way. Like Dorothy in *The Wizard of Oz*, you may start out timid and unsure of yourself, but with each step on this golden path of self-awareness you gain the confidence, courage, and power to go forward.

Believe that there's more to you than your reflection in the mirror. Go beyond your appearance, your roles, and your titles to connect with the part of yourself that has a limitless capacity for greatness. "Know Thyself" and you will discover the key that leads to enormous success.

33 Principles To A G.R.E.A.T. Life

Principle 16:

A G.R.E.A.T. person engages in self-discovery.

Day 17

Awareness

"Watch your thoughts; they become words.
Watch your words; they become actions. Watch
your actions; they become habits. Watch your
habits; they become character. Watch your
character; it becomes your destiny."

– Lao-Tze

"People are getting it: Being aware of
the moment is what matters most. It's
transformative. It redefines what it means to be
alive."

– Oprah

The most powerful moment is the present moment.
Why? Because it's all you'll ever have. Think
about it: Right now it's...Now. 10 minutes
from now will be...Now. 365 days from now will be
(you guessed it!)...Now. A lot of things we put off until

tomorrow never get done, because tomorrow never really comes. Unfortunately, we are living in the age of the time chasers. Many of us have hectic schedules, rushing to do this or that. There is little regard for honoring the present moment.

At some point, we're all guilty of focusing too much on the past and future. It's okay to look back to learn valuable lessons or to look forward to plan effectively, but not enough acknowledgement of the present moment will have you walking around like the living dead. How many times have you gone to a grocery store or on an errand and realized as you got in your car that you couldn't remember anything that just happened. It was all a blur. Many times I could not remember my entire day. The scary thing is, if you're not careful, you may find yourself living in an orb of unconsciousness, and your whole life will pass you by.

> "Many of us have hectic schedules, rushing to do this or that. There is little regard for honoring the present moment."

Lack of awareness can cause us to make so many unavoidable mistakes. You're late for an appointment because you couldn't find your keys; you lose money because you weren't paying attention to a transaction; or you gain several unwanted pounds because you're not mindful of your portion sizes or how many of those cookies you ate. Being unaware can also cause you to miss out on opportunities. Not just professional opportunities, but opportunities to share quality time with loved ones as well.

Several years ago when I began practicing awareness, one of the first things I noticed was the interaction between my boyfriend and I at the dinner table. It was the saddest thing, but I noticed we were both eating with our heads down, occasionally looking up to stare off into space, obviously caught up in our thoughts. I wondered, how long has this been going on? More than likely from the beginning, but it was an eye-opener. We were both busy entrepreneurs with hectic travel schedules and little time to spend together. I became more aware in our quality time and the shift in consciousness has enhanced our relationship.

"Learn how to turn off and bring your attention back to the present moment. What's in front of you right now? That's the most important thing."

In our society we have become chronic multi-takers, especially women. Before we get out of bed and place our feet on the floor, our minds are already racing. Learn how to turn off and bring your attention back to the present moment. What's in front of you right now? That's the most important thing. That's the only thing you can do at this moment, so give it your fullest attention. No doubt this is a challenge. Living in the present takes consistent effort. The more you practice and make it a habit the easier it becomes.

When we are living in the moment we come alive. We

are able to go beyond the surface of things and make a real connection. Living in "the Now" allows us to experience a release and a freedom that is the essence of higher living. We become open to an abundant level of peace and happiness and our lives are transformed by the discovery. Indeed, there is power in awareness!

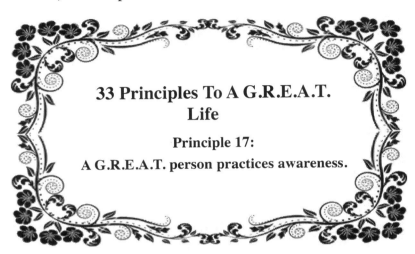

33 Principles To A G.R.E.A.T. Life

Principle 17:

A G.R.E.A.T. person practices awareness.

Day 18

The Power of Your Mind

"Would you like to experience more power? Develop your power consciousness. More health? Develop your health consciousness. More happiness? Fill your consciousness with happiness…Live the spirit of these things until they become yours by right. It will then become impossible to keep them from you."

– Charles Haanel

"We become what we think about most of the time."

– William James

"If you can control a man's thinking, you don't have to worry about his actions."

– Carter G. Woodson

Your mindset is the battery that powers your life. You can't think ordinary thoughts and expect to have an extraordinary existence. Success takes shape in the mind first, so it's important to elevate your mind above the base level of thinking. As author Dennis Kimbro says "Man never reaches heights above his level of thought."

The real work in overcoming any obstacle is done in the mind, because limitations only exist there. As we begin to raise our level of thinking, our new consciousness shines light on these "limitations" and exposes them as the illusions they really are. With this newfound freedom, you will be amazed at what you can do. There are things I have accomplished simply because I had no clue it was impossible. I call this the "Wile E. Coyote Factor." This Looney Tunes character is well-known for his relentless pursuit of the Road Runner. He is so intent on catching his prey that at times he runs completely off a cliff into thin air. Wile E. Coyote is just fine until he realizes that it's impossible to walk on air, then he falls. The

"When you are sure of your vision and clear in your intentions, keep on running."

lesson here is that you will always achieve what you believe you can. Just don't look down! When you are sure of your vision and clear in your intentions, keep on running. Turn away from information that attempts to verify that what you are trying to achieve is impossible and abnormal.

Maybe it's time that you created a new normal. Living a great life is when you make the uncommon common and when the supernatural becomes a natural occurrence. Train your mind to believe that it is strange to live an unfulfilled life. Get to the point where you are unable to comprehend living beneath your potential. Believe that there is only one way to live, and that's successful, on your own terms.

"Out of sight, out of mind" is a common and true belief. However, I think that "out of mind, out of sight" is more accurate. The things that show up in your life are a direct result of your mind activity. If you ever want to know what you've been thinking, just take a look at your surroundings. Likewise, if there are things in your life that are absent, then develop a consciousness of what it looks like. This is the master key to manifestation.

For example, if you want to be wealthy, observe wealthy people. Ask yourself: How does a wealthy person spend their time? How do they think? What do they do for a living? Where do they go for entertainment? Gather information to create a complete picture in your mind of a wealthy lifestyle. As you retain that visual image, begin to align your actions, attitudes, and habits with what you want.

I *love* watching *MTV Cribs* and *E!'s Fabulous Life Of* series. I'm not merely watching for my entertainment, I'm taking notes. I want to get tips and ideas on how high-achievers operate in business, how they invest their money, and how they maintain their lifestyle. Because I understand the Universal Law of cause and effect, I create an image of what I want in my mind, because I know if I can build it in the spiritual world (cause), I can have it in the physical world (effects).

Sometimes in our lives we are unable to move forward because we are trying to do new things with an old mentality. We are trying to pour new wine into old wineskins (Mark 2:22). But greatness is a mind set, happiness is a mindset, heath is a mindset, wealth is a mindset. In other words, *get your mind right*. How you think will determine who and what you shall become.

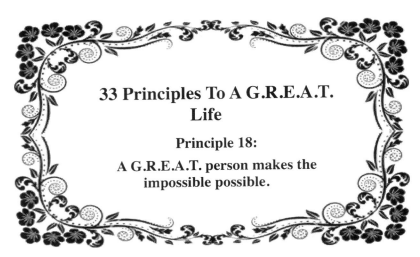

33 Principles To A G.R.E.A.T. Life

Principle 18:

A G.R.E.A.T. person makes the impossible possible.

Day 19

Get Knowledge

"Study the great and become greater!"
– Dennis Kimbro

"Education's purpose is to replace an empty
mind with an open one."
– Malcolm S. Forbes

"Readers are leaders."
– Dennis Kimbro

The old adage "knowledge is power" is so common that it's often overlooked. But the importance of learning cannot be overstated. Expanding your mind enhances every aspect of your life. It's an essential tool that will take you from good to great. All knowledge can be useful, but knowledge of the past is invaluable to living the life of your dreams. When we learn from the greats that came before us, we use their lives as a foundation to become even greater. We can glean from them and go further because they have lived and paved the way.

Great people are readers. They know that enormously successful people always leave a trail that can be found, most often, in a book. Between the two covers, you can find a map to greatness from the most extraordinary people that ever walked this earth. In this light, reading can be a creative way to secure a good mentor when you can't find one close by. The public library is free and there you have access to thousands of mentors; take your pick.

When I'm feeling sorry for myself and need a little boost or pep talk about hard work, I reread *Up From Slavery* by Booker T. Washington. It is really hard to complain and wallow in my miseries when I read how Washington started the Tuskegee Institute from the ground up with little money and all the odds stacked against him. His words come across like advice from an uncle who has lived an extraordinary life. As a matter of fact, I refer to him as Uncle Booker T! No, I'm not crazy. I just know that when we stand on the shoulders of the sages and ancestors, and apply their words of wisdom, we can propel ourselves further faster.

The great scientist Albert Einstein said, "Intellectual

> "Great people are readers. They know that enormously successful people always leave a trail that can be found, most often, in a book."

growth should commence at birth and cease only at death." He's right. A great person never stops learning and growing. They're on fire for transformative information or advice. They acquire facts about their industries, new societal trends, technology, and ways that they can improve their lives. They are constantly feeding their minds and applying the knowledge. As a result they experience tremendous personal growth, making a quantum leap into excellence.

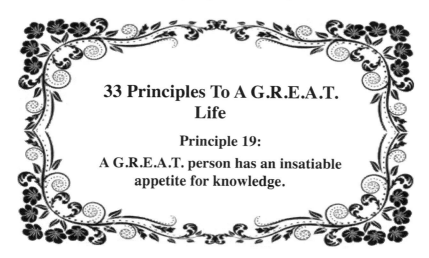

33 Principles To A G.R.E.A.T. Life

Principle 19:

A G.R.E.A.T. person has an insatiable appetite for knowledge.

Day 20

Dream Big Dreams

"Make no small plans for they have no power to stir the soul."

– Niccolo Machiavelli

"Dreams are renewable. No matter what our age or condition, there are still untapped possibilities within us and new beauty waiting to be born."

– Dale E. Turner

"Dreams are illustrations from the book your soul is writing about you."

– Marsha Norman

In pageantry it's a common practice for each contestant to chose a "life's philosophy" as part of their introduction speech. Mine would always be, "Shoot for the moon because even if you miss, you'll still land among the stars." It's true. A high aim that misses the mark will leave you in a better place than a low aim that hits the target. In order to live the great life, it's vital that you think big thoughts and dream big dreams.

Some people are afraid to dream big because they fear failure. They allow doubt to come in and convince them that their plans won't materialize. The size of the vision can be pretty intimidating, but I've never met a person who persisted towards a goal that didn't eventually reach it. As we covered in "Be Resilient," failure is a part of the process of greatness, so there's nothing to fear. You should expect obstacles and setbacks somewhere along this path, but remember you can *overcome* them.

I'm pretty sure if you stood at the base of the Great Pyramid of Giza the size is pretty intimidating. It is the only one of the seven wonders of the ancient world that is still fully intact. It's also the oldest and largest pyramid in that region. If you've ever seen a picture of this awesome structure, the tourists at the bottom look like ants! As massive as the pyramid is, it was built with much, much smaller stones and took 20-plus years to complete. Like the phenomenal pyramid of Giza, every forward step you take toward your vision will lead to immense greatness. Excellence is not an overnight process. It's the result of accumulated progress. Even the baby steps add up. The point of doubt is where you really have to put faith to work knowing that if you can think it, it's possible. Every great achievement was first a big dream in the mind of that individual.

As a child, I enjoyed playing the game of "make-believe" with my friends. We would dress up in my grandmother's clothes and pretend that we were rich and famous people. We talked about how fabulous and carefree our lives were. We bragged about our mansions and expensive cars, our famous friends and the movies we starred in. We would go on like this for hours. When the game was over we would put the clothes back on the hangers, put the heels back in their place, and the jewelry back in the jewelry box. Then we were off to play freeze tag, hopscotch, or double-dutch. I remember lingering behind as my friends went outside to play. "Make believe" was a favorite childhood game, but now as an adult I look back on those times and realize that it was not a game to me. I could never get over my childhood fantasies of living a life of great significance, abundance, and influence. My friends were playing, but I was practicing.

I have learned that there's an art to dreaming big. As with all good things, you have to apply balance and moderation. There were times when I would spend so much energy imagining my big dreams that I would begin to feel stressed out and weary. I found myself feeling overwhelmed because the "how" wasn't always apparent in the vision. I had to realize that my job is to keep the passion of the dream in my heart and focus on the task at hand. If you can't see how, just "keep your eyes on the prize" and position yourself for the next step. The things you need will always appear when you're ready for them.

I live a wonderful life now for many different reasons. However, the key reason is that I couldn't see anything else for myself but greatness. My dreams are so big that they leave no space for mediocrity. Remember: *Your mindset is the battery that powers your life.* If you're afraid to dream big you can't experience the abundance and fulfillment that is yours by Divine right. Free your imagination and don't hold back. Visualize yourself fulfilling your biggest desire. Believe in your grand vision and position yourself for take-off!

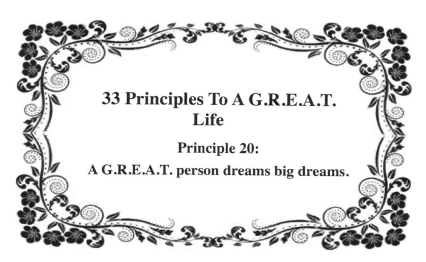

33 Principles To A G.R.E.A.T. Life

Principle 20:

A G.R.E.A.T. person dreams big dreams.

Day 21

Take Action

"If you have built castles in the air, your work need not be lost; that is where they should be. Now put the foundations under them."

– Henry David Thoreau

"For as the body without the spirit is dead, so faith without works is dead also."

– James 2:26

"Trust your instincts. And never hope more than you work."

– Rita Mae

You can dream big dreams, have the right intentions, read this book, attend seminars, webinars, conference calls, etc., and it all means nothing if you don't take ACTION. Real transformation occurs when you find your passion and then take the necessary steps to bring forth what you want. Think of it as if you were holding a winning lottery ticket worth 10 million dollars. Possessing the ticket would not be enough to become rich. You must take the proper steps to retrieve your fortune. Apply action to your plans and cash in on your power. Don't waste your potential by putting all of your energy towards dreaming.

Your daily actions should be aligned with your dreams if they are to come to fruition. Pay attention to how you spend your time and define which activities are unproductive and which ones are useful to helping you meet your goals. For example, when I decided to write and finish this book, I knew that I would need intense focus to make it happen. I set a date of completion and began to adjust my lifestyle to meet my deadline. I examined my to-do list from day to day and began to omit activities that were not contributing to my goal. Besides my book, there were four other activities that demanded my time. I ranked these in order of priority with my book at the top of my list. I was self-employed and I had to make a living, so priority two and three were activities that produced immediate income to support my household and fund my book project.

I began to break down how many hours I needed to spend a day on each activity to keep myself afloat and on target. I kept my work hours the same and tweaked my schedule to find the extra time to complete this book. I realized that I would have to wake up an hour earlier during the weekday. Tasks such as checking e-mails were slotted as an "end of the day" activity and only for 10-15 minutes. I usually spent an hour-and-a-half collectively every day checking my e-mail and Facebook accounts. I now needed that extra hour to write and edit. Also, I grouped all of my errands together so I only had to leave my home during the week for one or two days. I saved several extra hours this way and used the free time for writing as well. I stayed focused and within five months, I reached my target.

After you've defined your goal, look around you for ways to take action and get started immediately. As author Wallace D. Wattles says,

> "Your action, whatever it is, will probably be with the people and things in your present environment. You can't act where you are not, you can't act where you have been, and you can't act where you are going to be. You can only act where you are."

The right move towards your goal will more than likely pull you out of your comfort zone. It's funny, but the action steps that you're dragging your feet on are probably the most important ones to take. Reread Day 14 if you find that you are stagnating. Pull through so you can finish strong. Make huge plans for the future, but utilize this very moment to the fullest.

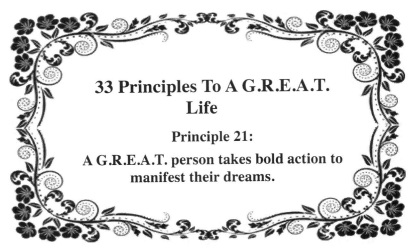

33 Principles To A G.R.E.A.T. Life

Principle 21:

A G.R.E.A.T. person takes bold action to manifest their dreams.

Day 22

Your Daily Bread

"People often say that motivation doesn't last. Well, neither does bathing… that's why we recommend it daily."

– Zig Ziglar

"Motivation is what gets you started. Habit is what keeps you going."

– Jim Rohn

It's hard to achieve today using yesterday's motivation. Like the manna that fell from Heaven, we can't feed ourselves with stale, day-old enthusiasm. With the rising of the sun, we must have a fresh dose of inspiration. It is important to create a life where you are surrounded by things that will help you stay empowered.

I start my day with at least 20-30 minutes of quiet time for introspective meditation and prayer. This is my time to connect and receive Divine guidance. Before I jump into my day, I check my monthly action plan for 5-10 minutes to stay on track with my personal growth.

I continue my day with effective action toward my goals. I love to read so I always keep a good book in my purse just in case I'm out and about and I find myself waiting for a service. I also subscribe to e-zines and newsletters from inspirational people who are aligned with my purpose. While checking my e-mail, I may open one or two of these briefly for a quick dose of inspiration. On my work desk, I have my favorite statues, trinkets, or quotes written beautifully on paper. On days when my schedule is tight and I can't squeeze in reading time, I listen to inspirational MP3s or CDs in my car as I'm running errands. Another common but great practice is having a vision board. The visual aspect is a quick and powerful way to stay motivated. My vision board reminds me of what I'm after and why I must keep going. It always reenergizes me on days when I'm in a slump.

This may sound like a lot, but it all flows well for me. We know that repeating the same things over and over forms a habit. Use the power of habit to serve you. I've tailor-made a lifestyle for myself that keeps me fulfilled, happy and productive. Because of the magnitude of my dreams, I must surround myself with positive things and positive people to stay consistent and in touch with my own power. I encourage you to do the same. Set yourself up for success. When you feed on inspiration daily, you become a motivating force to others. Remember, you are what you eat.

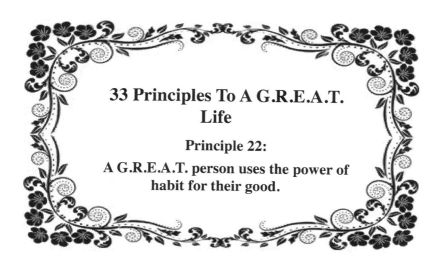

33 Principles To A G.R.E.A.T. Life

Principle 22:

A G.R.E.A.T. person uses the power of habit for their good.

PART IV:

Be **A**uthentic

Day 23

Are You Really Happy?

"Don't put up the walls. The same wall that keeps out disappointment keeps out happiness."

– Jim Rohn

"Holding on to anger is like grasping a hot coal with the intent of throwing it at someone else; you are the one who gets burned."

– Buddha

"Most people are about as happy as they make up their minds to be."

– Abraham Lincoln

Material and external things will never bring lasting fulfillment. True happiness is from within. When we really begin to pay attention to ourselves, our thoughts, and our reactions, we realize how often we choose anger and negativity over peace and happiness. It's so easy to be miserable, sad, and negative. It requires greater effort to be positive. Therefore, I came to the conclusion that happiness is a conscious choice.

Within all of us there is a light at our center called the "solar plexus." This center is the "sun of our body." It's the place where our life energy emanates. Positive energy brightens this light. Negative energy dims it. When this inner light shines brightly we experience health, prosperity, and good relationships. Great opportunities come our way. When this light is dim from negativity, we experience disease, disharmony, contention and strife. Like the sun in the sky that gives life to all things on this planet, we need the sun within us to shine bright for vitality, well-being and growth.

One thing that helped me find my happiness is realizing why the big-bellied Buddha laughs. He laughs heartily because he knows one of the greatest truths in life: *It's not that serious!!* At the end of the day, is harboring anger really worth the outcome? When you get sucked into someone's negativity, you give them your power. You become a slave to that person or situation. We show more strength when we can open our hearts and let go of the pain. With consistent spiritual development we are able to see the good in everything. We can decide how any situation will affect us instead of being at the mercy of circumstance. As we take control in spite of the difficulty, we truly own our power.

To be authentically happy you must clean your

emotional house. It's time to go within and deal with all the animosity. You may need to have a conversation with someone in order to release some pain and anger, but resolve from this point to express how you genuinely feel in the spirit of positivity (Ephesians 4:15). This can be hard to do, but you must do it for your own sake. You deserve to be happy, and harboring negativity may be the only thing keeping you from living the great life.

I have learned the hard way that when you build up a wall, you only end up hurting yourself. Holding grudges causes stress on your mind and body. All my life I have constantly entertained negative thoughts and harbored resentment and anger. It wasn't until a few years ago when I had a health scare that I began consciously seeking happiness. At the age of 25, I started having pain in my sides and my stomach. I noticed that they always seemed to get worse when I was upset or having one of my negative "episodes." After several doctor's visits, I was diagnosed with a peptic ulcer and a bad case of acid reflux. This was a major wake-up call. Years of anger and resentment were literally eating away at me. Being a student of holistic health, I realized that this was a physical manifestation of a spiritual problem of holding on to negative things. What's true in the spirit always manifests in the body.

Releasing the pain has been one of the most challenging things I have ever had to do. I realized that I wanted to hold on to this negativity. The ego, when it's tamed, can be a great asset, but the ego running wild can cause a lot of destruction. It loves to feed on negative energy. Indulging in the ego is like scratching an infected sore. The urge is strong and when you scratch it, it feels so good, but afterward you find yourself worse off than before. After my diagnosis, I faithfully took the medicine prescribed by the doctor, but I knew that true healing would come in the light of acceptance and living with a free-flowing heart.

Even though it is easy to be angry and resentful, the cost of these emotions is expensive. You end up paying with your life. You will either lose fulfillment or you may lose your life all together through stress and dis-ease. Know that anger is a product of unmet expectations. Great expectations of others lead to even greater disappointments. I have learned that it's wise to keep expectations high for yourself, and low for others. This allows you to love and accept them from where they are.

All the great things in life are on a higher vibration, and in order to receive them properly, we must shake off the negative weights that hold us down. Whatever has caused you pain and anger, address it and let it go. I have to tell myself often, it's not worth it. Instead of nursing the anger, throw back your head and laugh heartily. *It's not that serious!!*

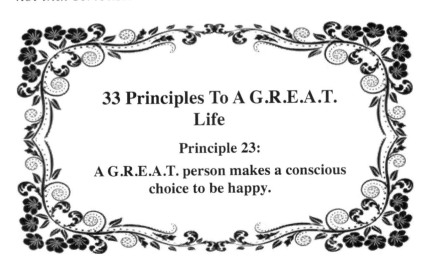

33 Principles To A G.R.E.A.T. Life

Principle 23:

A G.R.E.A.T. person makes a conscious choice to be happy.

Day 24

Take Off the Mask

We Wear the Mask

We wear the mask that grins and lies,
It hides our cheeks and shades our eyes,—
This debt we pay to human guile;
With torn and bleeding hearts we smile,
And mouth with myriad subtleties.
Why should the world be over-wise,
In counting all our tears and sighs?
Nay, let them only see us, while
We wear the mask.
We smile, but, O great Christ, our cries
To thee from tortured souls arise.
We sing, but oh the clay is vile
Beneath our feet, and long the mile;
But let the world dream otherwise,
We wear the mask!

– Paul Lawrence Dunbar

In April of 2008, I made the life-changing decision to compete in one final pageant system. I completed the application for the Miss Black South Carolina USA pageant and began preparation for the November show. For my 39th competition, I should've felt great ease vying for the state title, but it was the exact opposite. I was extremely nervous and felt completely off my A-game. For starters, this was my first pageant since November 2005. To be honest, it wasn't the three-year hiatus that made me feel inadequate. It was the transformation within the three years that had me unnerved. The growth I experienced since graduating college had led me to a more authentic place. I was truly finding myself.

Looking back on my pageant career, I realized that this was the first pageant I would compete in authentically. For previous competitions I had learned how to mold myself according to what the mainstream pageant world wanted. When I did interviews, I knew exactly what to say and how to say it to score high, whether it was authentic or not. I knew how to smile, walk and give the judges exactly what they wanted. I knew how to stay in my neat box to win competitions. I certainly experienced personal growth along the way, but I realized that this time I would bring myself first and experience next. It was like learning how to walk and talk again.

At 25, I knew I could not afford to waste any time being afraid, so I went all in. I took off the mask and I was open. At first I felt a little vulnerable and unsure of myself, but with each step I gained confidence. The mask was a crutch and I had to learn to walk without it. The beautiful thing is, when I took the mask off, I *flew*. I won the competition in November, and having made it through that experience I put myself in an eight-month pageant boot camp to prepare for nationals. Life was the Instructor. Everything I was afraid to do, instead of shying away from it, I went to it. I realized that sometimes fear is the arrow pointing you in the direction you should go next. I was getting to know myself and now it was time for others to get to know me too. The *real* me.

When I did newspaper, television and radio interviews, instead of telling stories that I thought people wanted to hear, I spoke from my heart. I calmed the fear of not being accepted with the fact that I accepted myself. To my joy and amazement, people loved it!! I learned that when you take off the mask, not only do you free yourself, but you have the ability to free others through your experience. There's no way you can make a genuine impact in the world smothering your light.

So when are you going to start living authentically? When are you going to take off the mask and embrace who you really are? You can't realize your greatest potential without personal authenticity. Sometime defining the reasons why we wear the masks is painful, but it's truly necessary. Lying to yourself may feel good, but as author Dennis Kimbro says, "Comfort is the enemy of achievement."

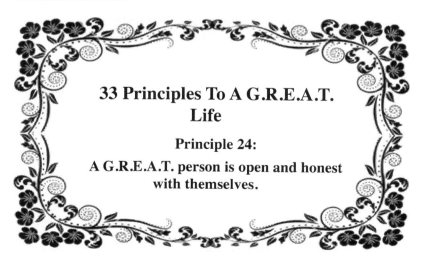

33 Principles To A G.R.E.A.T. Life

Principle 24:

A G.R.E.A.T. person is open and honest with themselves.

Day 25

Do You. Live Your Passion. Be a Light.

"Be who you are and say what you feel because those who mind don't matter and those who matter don't mind."

– Dr. Seuss

"Don't ask yourself what the world needs; ask yourself what makes you come alive. And then go and do that. Because what the world needs are people who are alive."

– Howard Thurman

Indeed. What the world needs are people who can light the way by being themselves and living their passions. By boldly going forth and letting your light shine you will inspire others to do the same. As I said, we all have a gift that can light up the world. When you're living for others, you stifle your light. At times when well-meaning people try to influence your actions, remember only you can decide what would be a good opportunity for you. Only you know inside what your dreams are. I have a rule: I only do the things that I'm most passionate about. If it doesn't move me, I don't care how good someone else thinks I would be at it, I don't do it. Part of going from good to great is knowing where your genius lies and pursuing it.

> **"Part of going from good to great is knowing where your genius lies and pursuing it."**

There are times when we do what we have to, until we can do what we want to. That 9-to-5 may not be your passion or the thing that allows your light to shine brightest. As a matter of fact, it may dim your light! But it's the thing that sustains you while you are building this great life. At this stage, make the decision every day to take at least one step toward living your dreams. That step may be spending 30 minutes every night after work to research your passion or making phone calls on your lunch break to gather the information you need to move forward.

When you go for your dreams and live from a point of passion there's a sweet essence that follows you. You will begin to glow. People will gravitate toward you because a beautiful radiant light is always inviting. Some people will begin to envy how you shine. However, they don't know all you had to endure, and the road you've had to travel to get to this point. The Truth is, they want their light to shine just as bright. Their jealousy may be a sign of frustration because they don't know where to start. You won't have to say a thing. Your illuminating presence alone will reveal the starting line.

> **"When you can embrace who you are and be yourself, you become magnetizing."**

When you can embrace who you are and be yourself, you become magnetizing. One example that comes to mind is James Brown. In the beginning of his career, his style to some seemed uncouth. When other artists and record labels were changing their style to increase sales, James Brown came to the stage raw, authentic, and unapologetic. When other labels were bringing in new writers and trying to scramble for new material that would appeal to an international audience, Brown drew people of all races, nationalities, and countries by just being himself.

It didn't matter if you could relate to James socially or not; his light was so bright, his rhythm was so infectious, and his spirit was so big. He allowed Divine creativity to flow through him with no interruptions. He shared himself authentically with hardcore human emotion and that was relatable. Maybe he really understood that music is a universal language. We all love, laugh, and cry at some point in our lives.

The really funny thing is, most of the time you can't

even make out what James is saying, but we LOVE it!!! It was James Brown's approach to really embracing himself that inspired the musical creative genius who we knew as Michael Jackson. Indeed James Brown lived his passion, let his light shine, and paved the way for others to do greater things. The moral of the story is: At every turn in your life, do you. Some of the greatest ideas and inventions were once ridiculous to others. Then the dreamer gave birth to the vision and the world reaps the benefits.

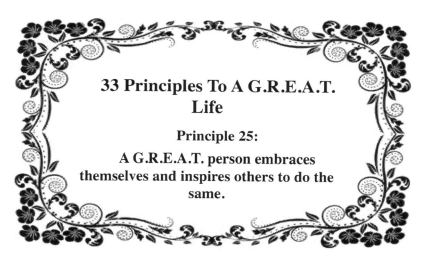

33 Principles To A G.R.E.A.T. Life

Principle 25:

A G.R.E.A.T. person embraces themselves and inspires others to do the same.

Day 26

Get Some New Friends

"Do not be misled: Bad company corrupts good character."

– 1 Corinthians 15:33

"What progress, you ask, have I made? I have begun to be a friend to myself."

– Hecato, Greek philosopher

"It is said in ancient scriptures: The Truth will set you free. Free to do what? To amend your errors and pick up new disciplines. That's what the Truth is for."

– Jim Rohn

All humans hold the potential for greatness. We all have a Divine light that can be developed to serve a higher purpose. But, if you are going to lead a great life, you have to be careful of the friends you have and the company you keep. Now that you're becoming more authentic, taking off the mask, enjoying true happiness, and letting your light shine, it's critical that you pay attention to who you align yourself with. Some friendships will naturally grow apart. As you move higher, some friends are going to feel uncomfortable in your light. Likewise, you'll be uncomfortable in their darkness. While you're making changes and adding more positive and fulfilling relationships, may I suggest two much-needed ones?

The Truth and Yourself

As I consciously started on my journey to greatness I realized that I had to make Truth my best friend. Truth will always give you the right perception, and the right perception is invaluable to building a great life. Lies stunt your growth, so we only harm ourselves when we reach for anything less than honesty.

No matter where you are in your life, awareness of the Truth is the starting point of restoration. If you are honest with yourself and committed to improvement, there is no limit to the things you can achieve. I have had the experience of watching well-meaning, good-hearted people live their entire lives below their potential because they refused to embrace the Truth. We all have aspects of our past that we wish we could change. But if we pretend those things didn't happen, then we really rob ourselves of learning the lessons that will move us forward. Instead of glossing over past mistakes, acknowledge what happened, learn from the experience, and embrace better character and judgment in the present.

To be successful, you must also develop a friendship with yourself. It will alleviate many common problems. It's harder to abuse yourself with overindulgence of any kind. Notice I used the word harder. Building the best relationship is a process and gets better with time. When I have to tell myself the stern truth, it's always in a loving manner. I don't yell or fuss at myself because I wouldn't do that to a friend. I'm patient with my personal growth and I take breaks and much-needed rest regularly.

I understand that how I treat myself determines how others will treat me. If I'm inconsiderate to myself, others will be inconsiderate to me. If I disrespect myself, others will disrespect me. I believe that the person who looks back at me in the mirror is worthy of love and respect and deserves every good thing that life has for her. I give myself the best, and it's no wonder that I'm constantly surrounded by others who only give me their best.

People ask me for advice quite often, but the truth is they already have the answers they need. There's nothing wrong with seeking counsel because the right people

> "Sound advice can help you make the right decision, but don't forget to trust yourself because the Truth lives in you."

can help bring clarity to a situation. Sound advice can help you make the right decision, but don't forget to trust yourself because the Truth lives in you. It's commonly called our "first Mind"- that still small voice that says to you..."this is the way, walk ye in it." (Isaiah 30:21)

Life is speaking to you, but are you willing to listen? When I received The Vision years ago, I looked over my past and realized I was an entrepreneur all along. I had to be honest with myself about why I wanted to be an attorney. I wanted it because I thought it would look and sound good. I wanted the image of what I thought was success. I could've wasted a lot of time and money following a lie, keeping up appearances, and living superficially. Instead, I chose to be real with myself, because if you can't be honest with yourself, then who can you be honest with?

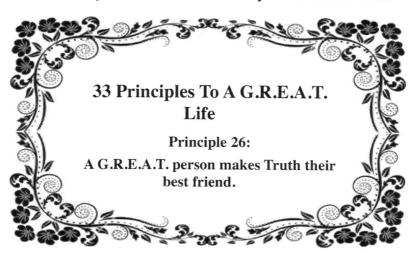

33 Principles To A G.R.E.A.T. Life

Principle 26:

A G.R.E.A.T. person makes Truth their best friend.

Day 27

The Power of Perception

"What the eyes report is determined by what the mind believes."

– Eric Butterworth

"Do not judge according to appearance, but judge with righteous judgment."

– John 7:24

"But be transformed by the renewing of your mind."

– Romans 12:2

In the name of modern living, we've forfeited the ability to make genuine connections with people in our surroundings. We commonly hold preconceived opinions and make snap judgments of others. But the right way of seeing things can never be found on a superficial level. The right perspective requires us to elevate our minds to get the full view and higher meaning of a situation. I strongly believe that wrong perception is the key reason for world wars and strife on this planet. Evil finds an entrance through limited minds that are resistant to change and driven by fear. Hitler is the perfect example of this.

It's often said that we perceive according to what we believe. When we learn to look at things not just with our physical eyes but also from the spiritual eye then what we believe will change. We must breathe new life into the old adage: Never judge a book by its cover. I admit that I have been extremely guilty of judging others quickly, but I'm learning. This is a challenge, but it is beneficial for us to practice this principle and make it a habit.

An exercise I use quite often is silence. Some days when I know I'm feeling edgy and a little off my center, I talk less. Instead of making a snap judgment about someone's character or actions, I simply remain a silent observer of the situation. I am always happy that I didn't express my opinion, because it wouldn't have been the right thing to do. At some point in our lives, we all tend to have knee-jerk reactions to circumstances, but the next time you're about to react on impulse stop and remain quiet. "Judge not according to appearances." Put yourself in that person's shoes, even. This practice deepens spiritual insight and heightens understanding.

It's always necessary to rise above your situation

in order to look at it from all angles. I've learned by experience that complete knowledge is six-sided and three-dimensional. When I really want to understand something, I analyze it from the front, back, right, left, top and bottom. You can't live on a higher spiritual plane viewing life from a two dimensional perspective. New ideas can't flow through a stale approach. The best and brightest opportunities are found by people who have clear perception. So when you find that your views are becoming fixed and stagnated, open the window of your mind and let some fresh air in. Renew your mind and be transformed.

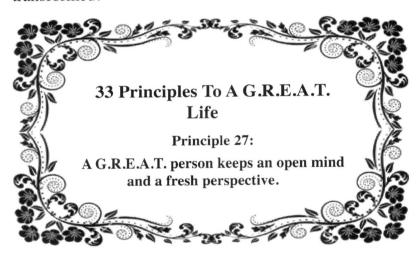

33 Principles To A G.R.E.A.T. Life

Principle 27:
A G.R.E.A.T. person keeps an open mind and a fresh perspective.

PART V:

Trust Divine Timing

Day 28

Seasons

"To everything there is a season, a time for every purpose under heaven."
– Ecclesiastes 3:1

"Times change and we must change with them."
– Christoph Cellarius

At every turn we must learn to respect the season of life. We have to close one chapter if we want to start a new one. If we are to experience all that Life has for us, we must do the right thing even when we don't want to. Letting go can be painful, but it's easier when we form a habit of *acceptance*. In these difficult times, you can take comfort in knowing that what hurts now makes for a really great story later! The new season brings you one step closer to living the life of your dreams. This is an excellent opportunity to give birth to a better you, so take advantage of it. You deserve nothing but the best, so love yourself enough to reject the good and have faith that the great is on the way.

Years ago, I had a friend who got a divorce from an unfruitful and abusive marriage. Although the relationship was over, she was so absorbed in the role of "wife" that she found it difficult to take off her ring. I wondered if she knew her true worth would the ring still be there. The season had changed and she still wanted to cling to what was familiar. As tough as it may be, you must find the courage to let go. You can discover your place in all of life's seasons. Don't reduce yourself to being defined by a previous period. Being out of season looks as ridiculous as wearing a bomber jacket in August weather. Life will keep moving so you have to keep moving as well.

> "You can discover your place in all of life's seasons. Don't reduce yourself to being defined by a previous period."

Clinging to the past is one thing, but acting prematurely can also cause a lot of unnecessary pain. The right thing in the wrong season can be a disaster. However, exercising discernment will allow you to determine when you must calmly wait or boldly go forth to experience the fulfillment you desire. Instead of letting anxiousness get the best of you, be patient and give the fruit time to ripen. Don't worry about being empty while you wait. When you're engaged in personal development there's always something to feed on. When

128

you're planting seeds consistently and continually, it's always harvest time.

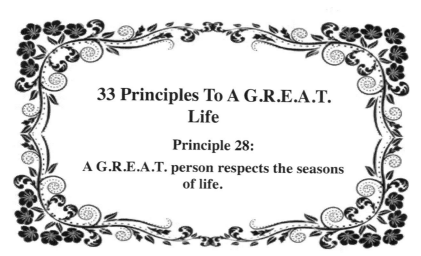

33 Principles To A G.R.E.A.T. Life

Principle 28:

A G.R.E.A.T. person respects the seasons of life.

Day 29

Use Your Time Wisely

"Time is what we want most, but what we use worst."

– William Penn

"Time equals life; therefore, waste your time and waste your life, or master your time and master your life."

– Alan Lakein

One of the greatest resources we have is time. How we spend this precious commodity today determines our future. Some say that time is just an illusion, and to some extent this is true. But at face value, you only get 24 hours a day, 168 hours a week, 8,760 hours a year; so use your time wisely.

I study the greats often and I've learned that they are

efficient people. They streamline their efforts to get the most out of their day and their life. According to Webster's Dictionary, "streamline" means "to alter, to make more efficient and simple; to organize; to simplify." I keep a copy of this definition on my desk because I realized that this is the way to achieve the things I want and maintain balance.

The past financial crisis provided a wonderful opportunity for purging excess and repositioning to get back to the core of what's most important. It was a pruning phase that resulted in mega growth for the people who were open to this form of Universal correction. It is possible to have the professional success you desire and have enough free time to enjoy activities with the people you love. Begin by getting rid of excess and minimizing waste. Recycling your plastics is not the only way to live green! We should be utilizing our natural resources responsibly in every area of life.

Great people are not just hard workers, they're smart workers. Nowadays, my business mantra is: "Work smart, play hard." Working long, grueling hours alone is not the key to living the life of your dreams. Doing the right things with the time you have is. There are periods in our lives where we have to be in "hustle mode" to achieve a goal, but too many of us are living this way. Before we can complete one thing, we find another activity to pile on our overwhelmed to-do list. Eventually, we began to feel out of control and then we realize that in our pursuit of the great life, we have become a slave to our dreams. Or maybe we have allowed other people to make demands on our time that pull us away from the things that matter most to us. We have to get really good at saying no to opportunities that are not aligned with what we want.

The definition of a great life is different for all of us. The best thing you can do is get intentional and clear about what a great life means to you. For me, it is being CEO of a thriving business empire, being a devoted and attentive mom and wife, having the freedom to travel the world in comfort with my loved ones, and experiencing all that life has to offer me. Sounds like a lot, but by streamlining and using my time wisely, it's possible.

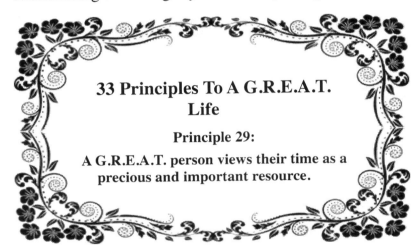

33 Principles To A G.R.E.A.T. Life

Principle 29:

A G.R.E.A.T. person views their time as a precious and important resource.

Day 30

When the Student Is Ready

"Finding is reserved for the seekers."
– Jim Rohn

"Keep on asking and it will be given you… he who keeps on seeking finds."
– Matthew 7:7-8 (Amplified Bible)

Life is a wonderful provider. It will always give you what you need when you're ready. As we grow and develop, our mind reaches another level of maturity. At this point, we are prepared for the next challenge. An opportunity comes along that allows us to expand our minds further. In ancient African history, this Universal Truth gave birth to the proverb: When the student is ready, the Teacher will appear.

The Teacher is Life itself, and can come in many forms. As with any noun, it can be a person, place or thing. For this reason, when you're on the journey to self-enlightenment you have to keep an open mind. I received confirmation to compete in my last pageant from a homeless guy at Piedmont Park in Atlanta who announced to a crowd as I passed him: There she is! Miss Black America! No, I never held the title of Miss Black America. I've never even competed in that system. But I was jogging through the park because I wanted to get clarity on whether I should enter another pageant. In oversized sweats, no makeup, and a cap pulled over my head, looking the complete opposite of a pageant contestant, the Universe gave me a profound YES to my question through a passing stranger's observation.

Because we are made in the image of the Creator, we believe that we are creators in our own right. To some extent we are correct. But the ultimate Truth is: We've created nothing because everything that can exist already does. Instead of creating, humanity is constantly engaged in discovery. Therefore, I believe that the best in life is reserved for the seekers.

Many people are afraid to search for the answer to life's mysteries. They resist thinking outside the box because they are afraid of being overwhelmed with the wrong kind of knowledge. But when you allow Life to be the Teacher, you'll never get more than you can handle. Every lesson comes in perfect timing. Life's instruction will always give you right knowledge.

There are many things I have found only because I sought it relentlessly. When I'm searching for answers and I come to the end of a road, I just close my physical eyes and open my spiritual eye. At this point, what was once a dead-end reveals itself as an unbeaten path. Years ago when I was building my grand vision of a billion dollar global empire, I began searching for efficient ways to live a fabulous and balanced life. I started by learning new forms of technology that saved time and energy. I created systems in my business to do the same. But at the end of two years, I found myself with most of the pieces to the puzzle and yet I didn't know how to pull it all together.

Nine months later, when I was ready, the Teacher appeared in several forms giving me the exact information I needed to carry out my huge vision. I realized that up until that time, there was no space in my life for this huge transformation. I had to finish my current lessons before I could graduate to the next one. A good parent wouldn't feed you another meal until you've digested the first. As they see you grow, they feed you more because they know you can handle it. The same is true spiritually. As you mature and open yourself up to greater possibilities, Life sees room to give you more. Then the Teacher appears... in perfect timing.

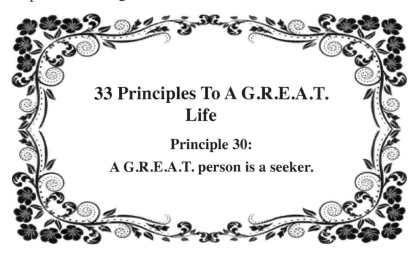

33 Principles To A G.R.E.A.T. Life

Principle 30:
A G.R.E.A.T. person is a seeker.

Day 31

When Opportunity Knocks

"The secret of success in life is for a man to be ready for his opportunity when it comes."
– Earl of Beaconsfield

"Don't wish for less problems, wish for more skills. Don't wish it was easy, wish you were better."
– Jim Rohn

"Success is where preparation meets opportunity."
– Zig Ziglar

Great lives are built on great opportunities. Knowing this, it is imperative that we are consistently growing and honing our talents and abilities to be ready when our break comes. When I want to go to the next level, I visualize what it looks like and then define what new skills I need to acquire for the mission. The truth is, favorable circumstances won't come our way until we become better than we currently are.

When we have been diligent in our preparation, we're eager to take a great opportunity presented to us. As good as it feels to be confident in our own abilities, we can rest assured that when we feel inadequate, Divine favor rushes in to fill the gaps. Remember: Your efforts pushed to the limits, wrapped in Divine power, will make you unstoppable. Your energy alone goes but so far.

Many times I've been asked to do things that I felt I wasn't qualified to do. A great opportunity would present itself and I feared I was not ready. But the Truth is, we are always ready to seize a life-changing moment. The Universe wouldn't bring it to you if you couldn't do it. Quiet the fears that well up inside of you. Yes, you are capable. You are smart enough, good enough, and more than enough to take that awesome challenge. Trust in Divine timing and take every opportunity with as much boldness and courage as you can muster. It helps to realize that the challenge is not about you. To find the power you need to forge ahead, shift your focus to all the people that will benefit from this opportunity.

It's really important to develop a mindset for expecting great opportunities to come your way. Amazing possibilities are all around us, but until we can believe this, we won't see them. The right mental environment will position you to receive offers that others think are simply impossible. Even in your physical environment, create a space in your life for good fortune. Wake up every day in anticipation of a phenomenal opportunity that will allow you to grow tremendously. To reach the height of your potential, you must take opportunities where you can stretch yourself and allow yourself to be stretched. Don't wait for perfect timing, embrace Divine timing without hesitation. You'll realize that just when you think you're not ready, you are.

33 Principles To A G.R.E.A.T. Life

Principle 31:

A G.R.E.A.T. person expects awesome opportunities to come their way.

Day 32

Divine Flow

"There's nothing more powerful than an idea whose time has come."
– Jim Rohn

"Ease on down, ease on down the road.
Don't you carry nothing that might be a load,
Come on ease on down, ease on down, down the road."
– The Wiz

I began the brainstorming process for this book in May of 2009. I decided on the title and began sketching the details of the format. I started thinking of all the components that make a person truly great. The first thing that came to mind was living on purpose. Resiliency was a no-brainer. At that point, I had the first two letters of the acronym G.R.E.A.T. After turning the idea over and over in my mind I came up with "empowered" and "authentic" a few weeks later. I finally had all components of G.R.E.A.T. but the "T". Nothing good immediately came to me, so I switched my focus elsewhere while I patiently waited for inspiration.

Three months later, as I was sitting on a chartered bus in Washington, D.C., the answer was revealed. It was pageant week at Nationals and I was exhausted from a day of appearances and rehearsals. As I was staring out the window, I heard *"timing: Honor Divine timing."* I laughed to myself. The very practice I used to get the missing link was the last piece to the puzzle.

Trusting Divine timing means going with the flow of life. In our society "going with the flow" typically means being passive and letting things happen to you in a way that makes you a victim of circumstance. But by going with the flow, I mean resist swimming upstream. There is a natural order of things. When we find it and operate through it, we step into another dimension of living. We can experience life in a remarkable way. There are still challenges when you're moving with the flow. Sometimes the current is rough and violent and we have to navigate the river of life like a white water rafter. But even in calm periods, we are actively engaged in the process.

> "Trusting Divine timing means going with the flow of life."

The other day as I was sitting at my desk I had a flashback. When I was in the third grade, I had a friend who was really great at the monkey bars. At recess time, I would watch her in amazement as she would clear the entire thing in half the time as any of the other kids. I studied her method. She had perfect timing on when to grab and when to release. She did this in a way that created a fluid movement with a perfect flow. I thought to myself as I was sitting at my desk: that's what living a great life is like. The key is being able to know when to grab and when to release.

Many mega-successful people operate in Divine flow. Oprah is a great example. I love reading about how she maneuvers from one brilliant idea to the next. Her decisions about her life path are not just intellectual. She *feels* her way. She is very sensitive to Universal shifts. She has a great sense of timing and knows when to grab and release. As a result, she has built a thriving empire doing what she loves. She may have her day-to-day challenges, but she is moving fluidly through life.

For many years, our world has been dominated by masculine energy. The need to control and conquer has led our planet to the edge of destruction and has turned our society upside down. But our world is changing. For decades some have been awaiting the return of the feminine principle to bring balance to our world. The feminine concept is the essence of Divine flow. It's about being receptive, intuitive, and having the power to manifest through non-resistance.

The wait is over. The feminine principle has been reawakened. It may take decades to produce global balance, but we see evidence of this return in the fact that people are beginning to desire more meaningful lives. As Mother Love is making her way back to the forefront we don't want to fight anymore. We no longer want the corporate power struggles. We are choosing understanding and peace over contention and strife. Closed and limited minds are becoming extinct, making room for bigger ideals and greater discoveries.

Once you experience the power of Divine timing you get addicted to it. You won't want to operate in anything else. It's complete perfection. Everything works out. There are many things I achieve with ease because I have such a great relationship with timing. Even in challenging times, it all comes together. I've never doubted the principle of Divine flow and I've never been disappointed.

I am finally learning how to dance with Life, knowing when to lead and when to follow; or when to assert myself and when to put a question out into the Universe and wait for the answer to bounce back at the right time, wrapped in perfection. I believe that the best thing we can do is to stop resisting and get in the Divine flow. There's no better place to be.

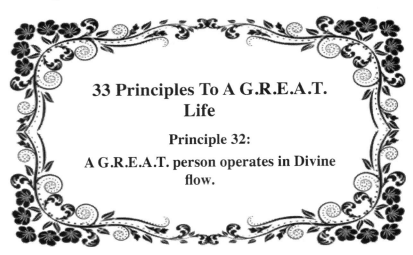

33 Principles To A G.R.E.A.T. Life

Principle 32:

A G.R.E.A.T. person operates in Divine flow.

Day 33

The Time Is Now

"Are you in earnest? Seize this very minute;

What you can do, or dream you can, begin it!

Boldness has genius, power and magic in it.

Only engage, and then the mind grows heated;

BEGIN, and then the work will be completed."

– Johann von Goethe

Today you've come to the end of this journey and tomorrow you will start another. But for now, forget about tomorrow, "for tomorrow will worry about itself" (Matthew 6:34). Now you have the knowledge to begin moving your life forward in a powerful way. What can you do at this very moment to implement these principles and began living the life of your dreams?

Every day we get to choose. Every moment we

are choosing. We can choose freedom over bondage, courage over fear, happiness over depression, health over sickness, abundance over lack. The choice is truly yours. If you are really in earnest about changing your life for the better then "Carpe Diem"- seize the day. Go as far as you can go *today*. Do as much as you can do today. This doesn't mean jam pack your schedule with a list of things to do. It means pushing forward and realizing that the new, fulfilled "you" is not a future concept. He or she can exist here and now.

> "We can choose freedom over bondage, courage over fear, happiness over depression, health over sickness, abundance over lack. The choice is truly yours."

You might have spent the last 20 years of your life in misery and lack or in a state of wishing and wanting great things to happen. You may have regrets of missed opportunities. You may feel that you've gone too far down the wrong track to ever live the type of life you've dreamed of. Know that there will never be a better time than Now to break free from this bondage of negative thinking. Shift your thinking to believing that you can, and you will.

The life of your dreams is calling your name. As you utilize these tools for success, you begin to elevate from a consciousness of fear to an awareness of power. With this new mindset you can confidently answer them back.

Take those dreams from the shelf and dust them off. It's time to stop merely existing and step into the land of the living. You owe it to yourself to believe again, because "it is never too late to be what you might have been." (George Eliot).

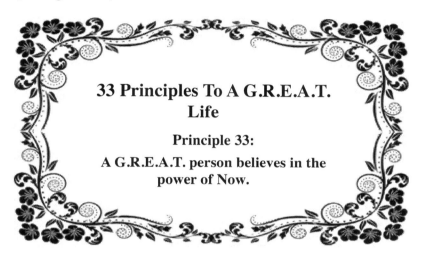

33 Principles To A G.R.E.A.T. Life

Principle 33:

A G.R.E.A.T. person believes in the power of Now.

Conclusion

Writing this book has been a journey within itself. As I reflect back to that day in May of 2009, I can't believe the incredible transformation that has occurred in just 10 short months. I've made so many self-discoveries along this trail, and I am truly changed forever...

I realized that as I was writing this book, it was writing me. I had to resolve so many issues that I have been carrying for too long. The same stories I shared within these pages were a source of comfort and encouragement to me on days when I was faced with heavy challenges. There were many obstacles that threatened the completion of this project, but as I allowed the Light of Truth to remind me of my Divine power, I was able to see that the "boogey man" was just a coat hanging in the corner. I wrote this entire book practicing the "Wile E. Coyote Factor" (Day 18). At times when I wasn't sure of myself, I just kept writing and refused to look down. For that I have gained extraordinary faith and courage for the journey ahead.

Three weeks away from completing this book, I began to experience swelling and numbness in my hands and wrist. It got worse every day. After a medical evaluation, I learned that I had symptoms of carpal tunnel syndrome. I use my computer regularly for business and marketing, but over the past 5 months, I had logged an extra 300-plus hours writing this book. I am predominantly right handed so the pain was stronger in my right hand than my left. At that point, I realized that I had two options: expand or retreat. I chose to expand. I took a week off, engaged in some holistic practices for healing my wrists, and finished this book typing and writing with my left hand. I utilized this challenge as an opportunity to rededicate myself to health and wellness, and my weekly yoga classes!

I was committed to seeing this project through to the end because I have a sincere passion to help others achieve the life of their dreams. I have so much I want to give to the world. As a child I realized that there's no reason for anyone to live defeated. My life-path is to expose people to the concept of life without limits. You can have your heart's desire if you are willing to stretch your awareness, elevate your consciousness, and apply the right principles.

This book is the cornerstone for the grand vision I see for my life. I thank you from the bottom of my heart for taking this journey with me. I pray that it has blessed you tremendously. I would love to hear your personal story of how your life has been transformed from good to great. Your story of empowerment and success could be featured on my website. You can contact me at:

Molesey Crawford
support@thequeencode.com
www.thequeencode.com

Here's to your extraordinary transformation and living the life of your dreams!

Acknowledgements

I have come a long way in my life, but not without the love, encouragement, and prayers of many people. First, I would like to thank my heavenly Father for unlimited possibilities and for patiently overseeing my personal growth these 27 years.

To my grandmother, Pearlie Mae Brunson, thank you for being a source of stability in my life and for teaching me the principles of diligence and hard work.

To my mother, Teresa Brunson-Nicholson, thank you for loving me unconditionally and supporting me 100% in all my endeavors.

To my dad, Charles Knox, thanks for your support in every way. I appreciate all the out-of-state trips to the national pageants.

To Josephine Bacote, my pageant coach and second mom, without your training, love and direction, I would not have my many crowns. Thank you for pushing me to be my absolute best.

To my mastermind partner and friend, Lori Pelzer, thank you for sharing your insightful tips that have transformed my life.

To Denise Clark-Wilson, thank you for being a shoulder to lean on in the last pageant of my career. You supported me tremendously and still gave me space to fly.

To Jerome Bryant, you called it right. A year before

college graduation you told me you met a woman who successfully owned multiple businesses. You said I would go on to do the same thing. At the time, I did not realize that you were giving me a prophecy. Thank you.

To my life partner, Carl Crawford, you believed in me and gave me a chance when you barely knew me. You placed me under your wing and protected me at a time when I needed it most. For that I am eternally grateful. Thank you for your undying devotion to my success. You are my best friend, and the greatest business partner a girl could have. I love you so much. Let's continue to grow together.

And to family members, friends, and even strangers who have touched my life in countless ways, without your influence, I would not be who I am today. May God abundantly bless you all!

About the Author

Molesey Crawford is a sought-after motivational speaker whose passion is to educate, enlighten, and empower others to realize their highest potential. She is a 2005 graduate of the University of South Carolina's Honors College and holds a Bachelors of Science in Criminology & Criminal Justice. After graduation, Molesey took a quantum leap of faith to pursue her passion in business and marketing instead of law. Molesey is currently the owner of Legacy of Timbuktu Publishing, LLC & Queen of the South Motivational Speaking, Seminars & Consulting. She is a certified representative of Compass™, a success company that gives women the courage, clarity, and tools to live the life of their dreams. Molesey is also the manager and marketing director of CMC Fine Arts, a visual arts company based in Columbia, SC.

Molesey grew up in a small community in Florence, South Carolina. Despite growing up in an underprivileged neighborhood, she managed to find opportunities that would propel her forward into a better situation. The more Molesey achieved, the more she felt a desire to inspire others to rise above their situations. Starting in 1999, Molesey began to use pageantry as an avenue to give back to her community. With a career in pageantry that stretches over a decade, Molesey traveled the state with her message of dynamic personal development, and was featured in various newspapers, magazines, television and radio shows.

Never despising the day of her small beginnings, Molesey empowers her audience to build a G.R.E.A.T. life one success at a time. Through her seminars and speeches she conveys the message that the power of positive change lies within us. We are all endowed with God-given power to change our circumstance and situations. The more you are aware of the power, the more you can utilize it and inspire others to do the same. Molesey resides in Columbia, South Carolina.

Works Consulted

1. Angelou, Maya. *I Know Why the Caged Bird Sings.* Random House, New York. 1997

2. Bible Gateway: **www.biblegateway.com**

3. Dictionary Online: **www.dictionary.com**

4. Haanel, Charles. *The Master Key System.* Atria Books Publishing, New York. 2008

5. Hill, Napoleon. *Think and Grow Rich.* Penguin Group, New York. 2003

6. Kimbro, Dennis. *Think and Grow Rich, A Black Choice.* Ballantine Books, New York. 1991

7. Kimbro, Dennis. *What Makes the Great Great.* Doubleday, New York. 1995

8. Morrison, Toni. *Song of Solomon.* Knopf Publishing Group, New York. 1977

9. Scott, Sofronia. *Doing Business by the Book.* Advantage Media Group, South Carolina. 2008

10. Think Exist Quotations: www.thinkexist.com

11. Wattles, Wallace. *The Science of Getting Rich.* Atria Books Publishing, New York. 2007

12. Williams, Terrie. *A Plentiful Harvest.* Warner Books, New York. 2002

Made in the USA
Columbia, SC
18 July 2019